"Marita Golden has written a brilliant, thought-provoking book. She voices the rage of brown and black girls who were taught to doubt their beauty . . . and she takes them with her on an emotional, transforming journey which celebrates self-love and self-acceptance. Ms. Golden is a healer, a griot attacking racism and self-hatred with wisdom, a lively spirit, and a generous heart. She encourages everyone to enjoy their days in the sun."

—Jewell Parker Rhodes,
author of *Douglass's Women*

"In this soul-searching, perceptive, and healing journey through the maze of the 'color complex,' Marita Golden challenges us to jettison the mirrors of the past, see ourselves through ourselves—and cherish the reflection."

—Paula J. Giddings, Professor of Afro-American Studies, Smith College, and editor of *Burning All Illusions: Writings from* The Nation *on Race*

Marita Golden

Don't Play in the Sun

Marita Golden has written both fiction and nonfiction, including *Migrations of the Heart*, *A Miracle Every Day*, and *Saving Our Sons*. She is the editor of *Wild Women Don't Wear No Blues: Black Women Writers on Love, Men, and Sex*, and the coeditor of *Gumbo: An Anthology of African American Writing*. She is the President and CEO of the Hurston/Wright Foundation, which supports the international community of black writers, and lives in Maryland.

Don't Play in the Sun

in the Sun

ONE WOMAN'S
JOURNEY THROUGH THE
COLOR COMPLEX

Marita Golden

Anchor Books
A Division of Random House, Inc.
New York

FIRST ANCHOR BOOKS EDITION, JANUARY 2005

Copyright © 2004 by Marita Golden

The Library of Congress has cataloged the Doubleday edition as follows:
Golden, Marita.
Don't play in the sun : one woman's journey through the color complex /
by Marita Golden.—1st ed.
p. cm.
1. African American women—Race identity. 2. Human skin color—
Psychological aspects. 3. Human skin color—Social aspects. 4. Golden, Marita.
5. African-American women—Biography.   I. Title.
E185.86.G625 2003
305.48'896073—dc21
2003053155

Anchor ISBN: 978-1-4000-7736-6

Book design by Jennifer Ann Daddio

w w w . a n c h o r b o o k s . c o m

Contents

Don't Play in the Sun

Scenes from the Color Complex: (My Own)

Ah just couldn't see mahself married to
no black man. It's too many black folks already.
We ought to lighten up the race.
—FROM *THEIR EYES WERE WATCHING GOD*
BY ZORA NEALE HURSTON

This society measures the progress for the Negro
by how fast he can turn White.
—JAMES BALDWIN

I am ten, standing before the gilt-framed mirror over the mahogany cabinet where the silver and good china are stored. It is seven-thirty and my mother, my father, and I have finished dinner. I have washed the dishes. My parents are upstairs in their bedroom. I stand before the mirror as I do almost every night when I have the dining room to myself. My head is draped in four long silk scarves that belong to my mother. Scarves held in place with a bobby pin at the top of my head. Scarves that are a seductive color-drenched kaleidoscope whose silk fabric kisses my brown cheeks as I imagine a White girl's hair must brush her skin—with the most awesome feeling of affirmation, beauty, and power. Standing before that mirror I am Snow White. I am Cinderella. My short, has-to-be-straightened-with-a-hot-comb hair has disappeared. My hands, like hungry butter-flies, are lost in the soft, imaginary tendrils that I see with a contented, dangerous stranger's eyes. With those eyes I convince myself that I can actually see the metamorphosis of the scarves into shoulder-length and even sometimes blond hair that frames my chubby brown face and that, at last, makes me real.

My mother, in a rare mood of satisfaction with my father, tells me, *"Your daddy is black, but he sure is hand-some."*

One summer afternoon when I am playing outside, racing the boys on our street to see who can reach the end of the block first (I do), my mother comes onto the porch and as I speed past shouts out to me, "Come on in the house—it's too hot to be playing out here. I've told you don't play in the sun. You're going to have to get a light-skinned husband for the sake of your children as it is."

———

In fifth grade we learn how to square dance and are assigned partners. My partner is Gregory, an olive-skinned White boy with raven-dark hair. In the center of the classroom, boys and girls face each other, giggly and jittery with anticipation. We nervously wait for the square dance music to begin. Gregory stands with a hand on his narrow blue-jeaned hips. His thin lips are curled in disgust at the sight of me. I am not the partner he wanted. When we square dance, we will have to touch. When we square dance, we will have to be close. I had liked Gregory until this moment, when his eyes calmly, purposely erase me and I stand squirming in my new dress worn just for this occasion. I glance down the aisle of boys, wondering who else could be my partner. When Miss Willis places the needle onto the record and the classroom fills with the sound of raucous, cheerful fiddle music, Gregory and I tentatively reach for each other's hands. We are reaching for each other across a centuries-old chasm of history and hate and hope and fear. When he touches my fingers Gregory jumps back and ostentatiously wipes his hands on the side of his jeans, as though now his hand will never be clean again, and walks back to his desk and sits down. I stand partnerless, exposed as what I saw in Gregory's eyes—not a girl, not his classmate, but a black and ugly and dirty thing.

Gregory didn't want to touch me, and there were boys I was afraid to touch. Boys like Russell in junior high school. Russell of the light "pretty brown" skin, and the "good" curly hair. Russell, whom all the girls wanted and who, on the occasions his glance slid over my face (quickly, never long enough to give me hope), made me feel invisible.

I was a tomboy and a daydreamer. I was shy around boys and people I didn't know but confident when speaking up in class. I didn't have a boyfriend in high school until my junior year. His name was Jose. He was Cuban, and a "redbone." Jose's parents greeted me with politeness but not much warmth the day I met them. I knew immediately that they thought I was too dark for their son.

Perhaps I began scribbling the first lines of this book on the slate of my unconscious on the near-tropical summer day that my mother told me not to play in the sun.

I don't remember my response to my mother's admonition. Memory is at best a mere suggestion, at worst a fiction we would bet our lives on. No, I don't remember everything about the day my mother spoke a series of words that were both edict and verdict. Words that nested beneath the tender flesh of my heart and that grew like the hardiest kudzu, impervious and confident, with a will entirely their own.

There is much that I don't remember, but I can still recall the shame I felt that my mother in one sentence had judged the worth of my brown skin (negatively), dictated the necessary course of my matrimonial future, dabbled into the murky world of genetics and DNA, became complicit in the psychological oppression that victimized us both, and reinforced the larger culture and my community's traditional command to girls who looked like me: "If you're black, get back."

Of course, back then there was no way I could articulate or comprehend the breadth of what my mother had accomplished by her words. Still, I knew I had been given a life sentence. But I am sure that to spite my mother and to assert my will, headstrong and stubborn, I continued to play in the sun.

There are so many words and phrases to describe African Americans' pernicious, persistent dirty little secret—*colorism, color-conscious, color-struck, color complex*. And then there are the more specific descriptive terms that separate Blacks and create castes, and cliques, and that are ultimately definitions not of color but of culturally defined beauty and ugliness, and that can end up distributing everything from power to wealth to love. *High yellow, high yalla, saffron, octoroon, quadroon, redbone, light brown, black as tar, coal, blue-veined, café au lait, pinkie, blue-black.*

But that day my mother spoke none of those words. She didn't have to, for by then I had absorbed everything I needed to know about color. I knew how deeply embedded was the culture's obsession with White-defined beauty, whether it was manifested in the icon status of Marilyn

Monroe or the light-skinned, "good-haired" Black women smiling from the cover of *Jet* or *Ebony*. *Ebony* and *Jet* were, in the years of my childhood and adolescence, the premier tabloid barometers of Black political and social reality. They were also a kind of scrapbook in which the masses of Negroes got to see proof-positive of the success and upward mobility of the most prominent members of the race. And while there were brown to black men and women profiled in these "bibles" of the Black community, it seemed to me that the Negroes who had managed to pull off the most amazing feats of achievement (Massachusetts senator Edward Brooke, Supreme Court justice Thurgood Marshall), those we referred to as "Negro Firsts" were usually light-skinned.

I was eight years old the day my mother warned me not to play in the sun and I already knew that I was invisible. I had not read Ralph Ellison's *Invisible Man*. Toni Morrison had not yet written *The Bluest Eye*. But already I had tasted the essence of racial and colorist tragedy. I feasted on it every day. I had parents who loved me, a nurturing family, many friends. I was smart in school, was often considered the teacher's pet. And I also knew that the specific physical traits that comprised my racial identity were despised.

Words had informed me of this. The words from family and friends that showered praise and compliments on lighter-hued, straighter-haired children for their beauty, words that I never heard used to describe me or other brown to black children. Words like "Isn't she so pretty?"

uttered with a sharp intake of stunned breath, eyes bulging in near disbelief at the sight of a curly-haired, light-skinned toddler. Words like "Just look at that hair!" (it was long, straight, thick), "Look at those eyes!" (maybe they were light brown or green or gray). All the words I heard. All the words I read. And for a long time, all the words I could imagine thinking or writing supported skin-color apartheid. As a child, I already knew that the world was a pigmentocracy. And I knew where I fit in that hierarchy.

In the 1950s I grew up in a largely segregated world. The only White people I came into contact with were teachers at school and a few fellow students in the even then majority Black school system of Washington, D.C. So I rarely heard directly from the lips of Whites words addressed to me or to other Blacks that assessed our relative beauty. But Whites had created another ongoing, invasive, and seductive and powerful conversation about beauty and color through movies and television and magazines and books and the collective imagination. And the language of that conversation was not only an echo of the self-hating dialogue among Blacks about skin color but also its progenitor.

"Don't play in the sun. You're going to have to get a light-skinned husband for the sake of your children as it is." Say the words silently. Listen to them and hear the anguished reverberation of the voice of three hundred years of mental suicide. The admonition is filled with so much fear, and so much dread. The sun, which is a symbol of life, growth, and power, in my mother's warning becomes a threat, a harbinger of danger. My mother's words were filled that day with

as much emotion as trembles in the voices of mothers today, warning their children not to play in the sun because of the fear of skin cancer. And yet for my mother, darkness, blackness, in its own way was a kind of disease whose progress, in its assault on me, she felt she had to try to halt.

I had seen the famous Coppertone ads for suntan lotion. I knew that White people worshiped the same sun that my mother warned me against. But I also knew that Whites' desire to possess a glaze of color in the summer did not mean they wanted to be Black. I knew that Whites could despise blackness and yearn for some measure of it at the same time.

I always had to be vigilant. Blackness, darkness, and its assumed resultant calamities could silently invade and possess me, even as I was engaged in innocent games of play. The threat of blackness hid, silent, waiting, even in the powerful lightness of the sun.

"You're going to have to get a light-skinned husband for the sake of your children." I was lost. It was too late to save me from darkness, but if I married a light-skinned man there was hope for my children.

My mother was well aware that the world attempted every day to erase me. She knew how little love lay in wait, how few open arms stood ready to embrace little brown-skinned girls with nappy hair and Negroid facial features. My mother had not constructed that world. Unable to challenge the beliefs about beauty and self-worth that she had inherited and that had shaped her attitudes, my mother strove nonetheless to warn me of the pitfalls and traps of the world she had not made but knew not how to destroy. From the vantage point of the present, I know now that those words, so harsh, and so brutal, were offered to me not as the punishment I heard but as an act of love and protection.

In the fall of my freshman year in college, 1968, I Afro my hair. For the first time in my life I love what I see in the mirror. I have never noticed the way my smile unfurls like a proclamation, the velvet depth and softness of my brows, the real color of my skin—a warm, intense brown. I realize I had never before looked at the face God gave me. I have spent years looking at my face through a swirl of conflicted emotions. Surely there must have been a time before this moment, before this day, when I looked at myself without judging, with acceptance. Surely. Surely. But I am a Black girl in a culture that convinces even the White girls I once fantasized about being that they are never quite enough. White, yes, but never ever thin or pretty enough. So how could I, a brown-skinned, unextraordinary (I have believed until now) girl with coarse hair, gaze upon myself as a work of art? Until now I have never before heard so many people affirm that Black is beautiful. And if Black is beautiful, I am too. Behind the locked bathroom door I sit on the rim of the tub, weeping for the perfect rightness of the face, weeping for the years I looked at it and decided not to look too hard. Never to look at it too deeply. Never to really claim it as mine. Black consciousness literally saved my life. The tide of history rescued me from a self- and culture-imposed sense of oblivion. The Black Consciousness Movement of the sixties allowed me to free myself from the prison of my mother's judgment that my color was a crisis, my color was a tragedy, my color was something to overcome.

Why do we remember the words of our mother more than any other? Why does a mother's assessment of her daughter resonate in the chambers of that daughter's heart like the Ten Commandments? Like the laws of gravity? Like a destiny that you simply cannot escape?

In college because I was Black and beautiful I made up for lost time. And it was in college that I became a color democrat. I dated Nigerians, Trinidadians, brothers from Harlem, from D.C. and Philly. I dated Howard University Black Power–spouting revolutionaries and working-in-the-system journalists. The men I dated, the men who were drawn to me, the men who became my lovers and my husbands, have spanned the color and racial spectrum. Color became incidental to me in choosing a partner. What was the man doing with his life when I met him? Where was he headed? How big were his dreams? That's all that mattered to me.

Color is in many ways an illusion. It is a game we play. It is subjective. We judge color not with our eyes but with our emotions. Our prejudices. Our longings. Our fears. Our hearts. My husband, Joe, considers himself much darker than I see him. Joe and I talk frankly and often about color, how it has affected us, how it affects our children, our family. I am often chided by my husband for what he considers my polarized views about color. We argue good-naturedly about his skin tone a lot. Insisting that he is only a tad bit lighter than me, he tells me I judge his color through the prism of my own color issues and generations of brainwashing. *He's probably right.*

A friend asks me why I am writing a book about the color complex, concluding, "Marita, you aren't even *that* dark." I don't tell him about my mother's words. I merely shrug and say, "Well, color, like everything else, is relative."

I am middle-aged, married, and Joe and I are one of twelve couples attending a dinner party at the home of a prominent D.C. lawyer. The house is beautiful, the food attractive in presentation and delicious. The conversation is ironic, humorous, informed, shifting between Black bourgie erudition and comfortable lapses into Black slang. We are doctors, lawyers, journalists, actors, writers. Nibbling on my salad of arugula, roasted red peppers, spring onions, and mushrooms, eyeing the rack of lamb and the wild rice that sits in the center of the table, I look around and see what I have seen all evening. I am the only brown-skinned woman in the room. All the other wives or fiancées or dates are very light to nearly white. All evening I eat and close my mouth and open my ears. These successful, witty, articulate people whom I find amusing and quite interesting betray no sense of color privilege. Still, I close my mouth, for I am too full of wonder that not one of the brown to black men in the room could find a woman who looked like me to marry. This is what I see when I skim the pages of *Ebony* and *Jet,* when I watch BET: the dark-skinned male power elite and their light-skinned trophy wives. I sit, mouth closed, as Joe looks at me across the table, worried, I can tell, that something is wrong. Something is. This is the personal love equation I have seen all my life. Black Power and Black Consciousness didn't change it. Remembering those days I recall that even then the female icons of the movement, Civil Rights to Black Power, were light-skinned Angela Davis, Rosa Parks, Coretta Scott King, Kathleen Cleaver, and Elaine Brown, who headed the Black Panthers for a time. Righteous sisters. My sisters. But Fannie Lou Hamer was too black and too angry and too country to achieve the icon status her sacrifice and hard work should have earned her.

I am not sitting here hating my light-skinned sisters,

but the clear and unmistakable color preference of the men of this "Talented Tenth" class has left me with no appetite and uncharacteristically little to say. Sure, opposites attract, but there's more than that going on here. I made peace with my black beauty a long time ago, but, sitting at the teak dining room table in a room filled with African and African American art, I am witness to a stark dramatization of colorism. I have been thinking and reading about color a lot lately as I ease into writing this book. So I know that what I am seeing has a lot more to do with power and privilege and economic status than with concepts of beauty. Because I have fought so hard to overcome it, I am probably more sensitive than most to evidence of colorism. But I am sensitive too because I have dared to think about it. I'm not afraid to talk about it, and too many of my brothers and sisters neither think nor talk about it. And I understand why. Who wants to go there? Unless you have to? But I have mourned long and hard the emotional price I paid for its effect. I see it everywhere because it *is* everywhere. People, especially the kind of people I am sitting with this night, like to believe that on the color complex "That was then. This is now." That colorism is a relic of the past. These are people who think they would never make colorist jokes or perhaps never tell their daughter not to bring home a dark-skinned boy. (I know that some of them would.) But the choices they make unconsciously and consciously support the color complex. Driving home, Joe and I talk, and he chuckles, chiding me, "You know how long and hard those men had to work to *be* doctors and lawyers? What kept them going was the knowledge that one of those women would be waiting for them at the end of it all as their reward. But let's make this a little more interesting," he says. "It's not just Black men who've got to plead guilty on this score. The really dark-skinned brother, the one who was the TV producer, the one with the big nose and the very broad lips and the glasses, how many dark-skinned women do you think would give him any play? And with the job and salary and status he's got, a light-skinned woman would be glad to have him. And no need to worry about the kids, thanks to her gene pool."

I am invited by a friend to a Sunday afternoon sistergirl networking party at one of D.C.'s trendier restaurants. The party is all women—friendly, confident, easy to meet and greet women—many of whom I don't know but connect with quickly as I stand sipping champagne and nibbling hors d'oeuvres. Seventy-five women fill the room, each at the top of her profession in business, the arts, education, mass communication. I am one of ten women of the seventy-five gathered who is brown to black. All my other sisters in the room are light, bright, or damn near white. I stand in the midst of D.C.'s Black female power elite. They anchor the evening news, are president of a Black-owned cable network, are discussing Hollywood options on books they have written, moan about not making partner at their law firms. These are the sisters to talk to if you want to make things happen. In this room, as I sip my mimosa, I conclude we could make a revolution if we put our heads together. But in this same room, the color complex and everything it signifies about how power and privilege is *still* distributed in the Black community is the ten-ton elephant in the middle of the room that we all ignore.

The color complex at its root is about words. The words we speak. The words we cannot. From the *Random House Webster's Unabridged Dictionary:*

> **black** (blak) . . . —*adj.* **1.** lacking hue and
> brightness; absorbing light without reflecting any of
> the rays composing it. **2.** characterized by absence of
> light; enveloped in darkness. . . . **3.** . . . pertaining or
> belonging to any of the various populations
> characterized by dark skin pigmentation. . . .
> **4.** soiled or stained with dirt. . . . **5.** gloomy;
> pessimistic; dismal. . . . **7.** . . . sullen or hostile. . . .
> **9.** . . . evil; wicked. . . . **10.** indicating censure,
> disgrace. . . . **11.** marked by disaster or misfortune.
>
> **white** (hwīt, wīt) . . . —*adj.* **1.** of the color of pure
> snow . . . reflecting nearly all the rays of sunlight or a

similar light. **2.** light or comparatively light in color. . . . **4.** for, limited to, or predominately made up of persons whose racial heritage is Caucasian. . . . **8.** lacking color, transparent. . . . **14.** auspicious or fortunate. **15.** morally pure; innocent. **16.** without malice, harmless. . . . —*n.* **20.** . . . opposite to black.

The equation is simple and complex. Light skin, "White" features plus straight hair equals beauty. Dark skin plus coarse hair equals ugly. *But,* dark skin plus long thick straight hair and "White" features can equal beauty. Light skin, "Black" features, and coarse hair equals ugly. There are so many caveats. So many footnotes to the clauses of the color complex. The precious treasure of light skin is like a charm; it works its *full* magic only in tandem with the complete arsenal of "White" physical traits.

Over a pre-theater dinner one night with two other couples, I talk about this book. The two other women are good friends of mine, both very light. For the rest of the dinner we talk of nothing else. It feels good. It feels like a baptism somehow. Just to talk about this dreaded subject. One husband asks if the color complex is as pervasive as in the past. He asserts that he feels there has been consider-able change. Joe and I then share anecdotes. Joe tells us about overhearing two girls in the math class he teaches at a D.C. high school talking about boys, and one of them saying that she would never date a dark-skinned boy. I tell them about sitting in my dentist's office and hearing a conversation between two young Black girls. One tells the other that she plans to go swimming that afternoon. She is tall, statuesque, very pretty, and very dark. Her lighter-skinned friend chides her, "Girl, you gonna git black." The dark girl laughs nervously, and shamefacedly insists, "I ain't gonna git black." Her words dig up my mother's admonition, and my heart breaks because of the self-loathing rippling through both girls' voices.

I am reading a book of poems by a friend. Several of the poems are about color. Her color. Or, rather, the absence of color. About being so light-skinned that the brown and black girls in her neighborhood regularly beat her up, chased her home from school. Accused her of being stuck-up and thinking she was better than they, because she was so light. She hated the girls because of what they did, and yet still wanted to be their friend. The girls beat her in a rage, a rage born of their fear that her beauty left no room for theirs. I call my friend and tell her how the poems touched me. We talk for an hour, trading color-complex war stories. I hear in her voice that she is still in some ways that little girl and that perhaps she will always be. I hear in my voice as I talk with this woman, feeling closer to her than ever before, that in some ways I am still the little girl

I was. Perhaps I will always be. No matter what I say or do. No matter how much distance time puts between that little girl and me. She tells me that writing the poems helped to heal some of the wounds, and then whispers, "But I still bleed sometimes." I tell her I do too.

Color: A Family Affair

I think there is probably as much difference between the life
of a black black woman and a "high yellow" black
woman as between a "high yellow" woman and a
white woman. And I am worried, constantly, about
the hatred the black black woman encounters within
black society. To me, the black black woman is our
essential mother—the blacker she is the more us she is—
and to see the hatred that is turned on her is enough to
make me despair, almost entirely,
of our future as a people.

—ALICE WALKER

I grew up in Washington, D.C., in a Black middle-class neighborhood of three-story, stately Victorian brownstones. My family, in the 1950s, was middle class in the way that many Black folks entered that economic bracket back then; my father drove a taxi and ran numbers (the lottery of that period), and my mother owned several houses in different D.C. neighborhoods, which she filled with boarders. This combination of entrepreneurship and enterprise on the part of my parents enabled me to grow up in a series of large, comfortable homes with working fireplaces and mantelpieces in the dining rooms, houses with mahogany wood floors that my mother covered with Oriental rugs.

Mine was also a home in which attitudes about color can best be described as schizophrenic. There was my mother telling me not to play in the sun for fear that I'd get darker than I already was. Yet when I drove around the city with my father in his taxi, or when he came into my room at night to talk to me before I went to bed, he told me stories I savored, of the Moors, the Black Arabs who conquered Spain, and the Egyptian queen Cleopatra, who my father told me was a Black woman.

I don't know if my parents knew it, or ever talked about it, but in the houses in which I grew up under their tutelage, their influence, and their spell, a war was being waged for my racial soul; and for much of my childhood, my mother won the battle simply because she had more troops on her side.

By the time I was nine or so I had internalized a kind of permanent ache, a persistent closing off and sometimes shutting down of my emotions on the issue of color. I knew by then that many people in my own community and most people in the White community did not consider me pretty, or valuable, or significant, solely because I had brown skin and coarse hair and clearly Black features. My mother's admonitions about playing in the sun and her ambivalence about my father's darkness were real. But in many other ways my mother constantly boosted and encouraged my sense of self. At the age of ten I was writing letters to the editor of the *Washington Post*, letters that were actually printed and that my mother clipped and proudly thrust beneath the gaze of visiting friends. I was an honor roll student and had already shown a gift for writing, and it was my mother who told me with a startling ease and assuredness that one day I *would be* a writer. Today, when I think of my mother's legacy to me, those are the things I hold on to in my mind, the recollections I embrace most fiercely.

But my mother, who grew up in Greensboro, North Carolina, possessed the kind of conflicts and doubts about the value of blackness common to her age and even our own. My mother was the color of polished teakwood. Born in 1908, my color-conscious mother might have been subjected to the paper bag test, a crude but oft-practiced ritual that prevailed for decades in the Black community. People submitted to the paper bag test would often literally have a brown paper bag held up close to their face, and if they were darker than the bag would not be admitted to parties, sororities, and even some churches. I know that when she arrived in Washington, D.C., as part of the Great Migration of Blacks from the South in the early 1920s, if she looked for a job in the classified section of the *Washington Post* my mother would have seen ads for a domestic worker (meaning Black woman), often with the words "Light-skinned girl wanted." But my mother was a very practical woman, and she was smart enough to know that in the world that she had not made but in which she and I lived *light was right,* and if there was any way for her little brown-skinned daughter to get close to that which appeared to ensure success and happiness, then she would advocate it.

Everything on television, in the movies, in the dominant culture, most of what I heard other Black people and White people say, supported my mother's colorist attitudes. So it was easy for me to walk through and live in the world as a child, making good grades and excelling at much of what I engaged in, while simultaneously knowing and feeling that because of my color the world, which on the one hand was so vast and so generous, could become in an instant small and stingy when I opened my hand. I could never be an actress because I didn't look like Dorothy Dandridge or Lena Horne. I'd never marry a rich or famous Black man because when I looked in the Black magazines I saw that they married only the women who looked like Lena Horne or Dorothy Dandridge. So I knew the score. My father, with his collection of books by the Afrocentric, self-made scholar J. A. Rodgers, his knowledge of Black and African history and tales of Black accomplishment, his bold, swaggering assurance (an attitude he adopted, he told me, *because* he was a deeply dark-skinned man, not in spite of it), was the exception, not the rule in my world.

I recall from my early childhood a profound sense of smallness and unease that often plagued me. In school we learned of the workings of nature, the planetary system, biology, and math. In all those subjects there was a logic and an internal sense of rightness that determined the outcomes. Colorism made no sense to me. But it was as undeniably a part of the world as the stars and the moon and the trees that as an energetic, rambunctious tomboy I loved to climb. It made no sense that just because of my color I would have to, as the ditty even I had chanted warned me to do, "step back" because I was black. It made no sense, but step back I did. I stepped back in my dreams at night to make way for the light-skinned girls. I stepped back in my fantasies, imagining the amazing and the unpredictable but fearing always that maybe only half of the fantasy would come true for me. I stepped back literally, in the presence of light-skinned girls. What was there for *me* to say? *Who* would listen? My mother had warned me about the power and prestige of lightness because she loved me, not because she didn't. That was the cruel, twisted logic that ruled my tiny universe. It was the logic that activated the larger world as well. My father's pride was years too soon, and by the time I became a Black Power baby and fully understood the depth of my father's racial pride and dignity, my parents were separated and I was estranged from my father.

I stepped back, but as I grew older—and even before Black Power/Black Consciousness and loud, wild, and long overdue assertions of Black self-love saved my life—I made lemonade out of the colorist lemons I'd been handed. Somewhere inside, beside the girl who stepped back, just in front of or maybe behind her shadow, there was another version of me that managed to root and grow and blossom.

I decided that if I had to be brown, and therefore unloved by the world, then I would simply be the smartest, the baddest-at-whatever-I-chose-to-do brown girl the world had ever seen. Everything the world despised I would use as fuel and springboard. And so my appetite to be the best, and to let the world that did not want to offer me a front seat know that I was here, that I was not going anywhere, sprouted like a tense, bulging muscle. My sense of outrage and competitiveness began to mute some portions of and chip away at parts of the smallness, chiseling out a territory inside me that was my secret. This was a continent where the rules were different and a logic that made sense prevailed.

My mother's first husband was light enough to pass for White. He was a gentle, compassionate man whose love for my mother was passionate and dedicated. Years after my mother died, one of her closest friends told me that Mr. Robinson was for much of his life tortured by the reality and the results of his biracial identity. His mother was White and he never knew his Black father. His mother had been cast out of her family when she broke the stringent racial taboo of that time. Like many lighter-skinned Blacks of that era, Mr. Robinson sometimes passed for White to neutralize the most degrading aspects of the rigid system of racial segregation or to simply get a good job that he would be denied if he revealed his race. He passed for White while serving in the army, a decision that exempted him from the effects of segregation and racism. But my mother's friend told me that when Mr. Robinson met my mother, my buxom, gregarious mother who wore white gloves when she went out to nightclubs and outrageous hats and stylish two-piece suits and clutched her leather or alligator handbags as though they held the keys to the secrets of life, she won Mr. Robinson's heart and he never ever "passed" again. But love was not enough for them. Mr. Robinson's demons and insecurities and his bouts with alcoholism doomed the marriage. One of my mother's closest friends, who became a surrogate mother to me after my mother's death, told me once about Mr. Robinson, "Ben was just all mixed up, and I think the root of it was his color, not ever feeling that he was really either Black or White."

Mr. Robinson had large, mournful eyes that neverthe-less presented a steely, unflinching gaze that seemed to have been honed by having witnessed and endured terrors that have a name and those we dare not even recognize. I remember as a child going with my mother to visit him during the worst bouts of her anger at my father. Mr. Robinson was a gentle man who doted on me and could sit as still as a monk, listening to my mother talk to him. Her voice, her recounting of the mundane, the extraordinary, the unexpected, nourished him as he sat quiet, still, shak-ing his head, clearly comforted by her presence. But I saw so much sadness in his eyes that sometimes I could not look at him and took refuge in the Nancy Drew book I had brought with me. With his massive shock of white hair and handlebar mustache, Mr. Robinson resembled a wizened Mark Twain. Sitting in their midst, watching him quietly listen to my mother the way my brash, often pompous father rarely did, I saw how much they loved each other. I did not know then why they had parted. I was still a child, but already I knew that here was another thing, love, that awaited me, that seemed to make no sense.

My mother, with quiet irony, told me once about when she met my father, her second husband: "I felt like I'd had a real light man and now I wanted to see what it would be like to love a black man." Even when my mother made this admission to me, as if confiding something that could explain the course her life took with my father, I heard the hidden yet still overt meanings of blackness and lightness. Loving my father, Francis Sherman Golden, was like loving a tornado or a hurricane. Their sexual union was so intense that my mother told me that my father made her feel like she could "tear up the house and put it all back together again." But they fought and argued with the same fierceness over money, who would own and control my mother's real estate, and they battled most bitterly over my father's other women. In Mr. Robinson my mother found a near-White man dogged by racial insecurities that destroyed whatever advantages were assumed to reside within light pigmentation and the life that it supposedly afforded. In my father, a man almost as dark as coal, she met, as her friends often said, "her match." My mother was strong-willed. My father was dominant. My mother was generous to a fault. My father was often an opportunist.

My father bristled with a sense of his own value and worth, entered a room like a peacock in full plumage, and when he hit the numbers spent thousands of dollars on custom-made suits and his car of choice, the Lincoln Continental—long, sleek, black, and unassailable. Surely the car was his alter ego. I've always felt that because of the relentless manner in which my father undercut so much of my mother's financial and material security, she raised me on two mantras: "Get some education because no one can ever take that away from you" and "Never let the left hand know what the right hand is doing." My mother utterly corrupted the biblical homily that urges humility as an aspect of charity. I knew without asking my mother, made cynical and bitter by her union with my father, that for her the left hand was *men* and specifically my father.

Still, I realized later that my parents were utterly united in their love for and devotion to me. My father raised me to be independent, to believe in myself, and I absolutely adored him. Yet even my father never told me that I was pretty or beautiful. That was one of the main tenets of the color code. Brown to black girls were rarely told they were pretty or cute unless their darkness was somehow mitigated by keen White-like features and/or long straight hair. But by telling me stories of Black men and women who had made history, shaped and changed it, my father united me with them, implied that theirs were deeds that I was capable of. My father made me feel valuable, which is a kind of beauty, when I rode in the front seat of his taxicab with him some days when I had no school. He took me among his friends—the men he shot dice with and whose numbers he collected, whom he jested and joked and jived with in the barbershop—and told them about my grades in school or a poem I had written, centering me as the focus of this male community. These men gazed at me with pride and acceptance. Perhaps the most important thing my father did for me was to raise me as if I were a boy, to take me into his world with no excuses and to expect me to measure up.

My father was the blackest man I knew and loved until I married my first husband, whom I was drawn to because he reminded me so much of my father. My father told me that the pyramids had been built by Black people. He was Black and he was proud. But my father's sense of completeness was so intense that for him pride was to be assumed; it was not something that one needed to shout. Black people were members of the human family, and as such had been kings and queens, slaves, inventors, had been defeated and had conquered. Their achievements and history, to my father, were to be taken for granted, and everything in the Black past made me the Black girl I was. I have wondered if he knew of my mother's conflicted feelings about color. Did he know? Did he care? I never told him of my mother's admonition to me not to play in the sun. She had urged me to marry a light-skinned man for the sake of my children. But she had fallen for my father, fallen hard, and my black-skinned father stole her heart. She never got it back.

My mother did not want me to get any darker than I already was, but she saw beauty in me in other ways. One evening when I was twelve, I was preparing for bed. I had just bathed and was standing in my bedroom about to put on my pajamas. My mother was on the other side of the room putting just-ironed dresses and blouses in my closet. She turned around and saw me standing nude and shivering. Suddenly she called my father, saying, "Goldie, come here." I thought I was in trouble and began to quickly pull my pajama bottoms on, but my mother told me to stop. When my father entered the room, my mother told me to stand up straight so that my father could look at me. I loved my father and trusted him completely, but all the values I'd inherited from society told me that for my father to look upon me at twelve, with this almost woman's body, was taboo. But for my mother that same act was necessary. For her. For my father. For me. And my mother was telling me to stand nude before him. As I tried to cover my pubic hair with my hands, my mother shook her head gently no and I let my hands rest at my sides. My father stood in the doorway of my bedroom, and what he saw was his daughter at twelve, my breasts beginning to fill out my chest, the waist that even then I thought was not small enough, and the hips I despised. But my mother narrated another body. "Your daughter has a lovely body," she said. My mother made me turn around so that my father could see my back, and my hips, which she praised as round and full. My mother stood near the closet, beaming with pride. I avoided my father's gaze for much of this extraordinary event. But when I was no longer shivering and felt my nudity sheltered by my mother's gaze and what I was afraid to see in my father's eyes, I finally looked at him. My father looked at my body with a loving father's eyes, seeing himself, his genes, his cells, his blood, his skin, in me. He smiled and left the room. That was one of the most vulnerable and sacred moments I ever shared with my parents, a moment in which they gazed upon my brown body, exposed, fragile, still forming, and blessed it. Together they turned my Black girl's body into a temple.

When I was growing up in the fifties and sixties, my hair was a burden. Plain and simple. There was nothing glorious, awe-inspiring, or confidence-building about my hair in my pre-Afro days. *And* it was short. Although like that of many African Americans my hair texture was in fact a mix of several strains, coarse and straight, the belief of that period was that it required straightening to make it manageable and "presentable."

Like many little Black girls I was *tender-headed.* Who wouldn't be, stationed between your mother's thighs, which held you in a viselike grip, as she used a comb to section off your hair, combing through a resistant terrain, greasing the scalp, brushing it, as you tried to escape. What an awful, terrible tug of war. My mother was like General Sherman marching through Atlanta when she combed and braided my hair. Like Sherman, my mother was determined to "tame" her foe. Like Atlanta, I swore not to give in. There was nothing soft, or tender, about her touch. Combing, braiding my hair was tough work, and not for the faint of heart. *Be still, stop squirming.* And my mother never seemed any more satisfied than I when she was through. We were both simply glad the deed was done.

And then, for all that work, when I went outside to

play, perspiration made the hair at the nape of my neck and around the hairline of my face "nap" up into tiny recalcitrant fists of hair that inflicted brutal pain when my mother tried to comb them out. I associated my hair with pain and dissatisfaction.

Until I Afroed my hair, every two weeks I went to the beauty parlor. I remember the acrid, sulphurous odor of chemicals, the warm, vigorous fingers of someone else washing my scalp. Then getting my hair straightened. Sometimes my mother straightened and curled my hair at home, and often burned my neck or ear in the process. So I'd have straight hair, but the price would be wounds and singed flesh. But all this was part of the color complex too—the need for "bone-straight," "pressed," "ironed" hair that beat back the genetic influence of our West African ancestors.

The Afro, the "natural," finally set me free.

And in the end my "natural" hair was soft, pliable, and beautiful. Left alone, freed from the angst, the torture, of the hot comb, left to its own tendencies and identity, my "natural," my " 'fro," sat on my head like a crown. I felt as if a weight had been lifted, and one had been. I had cast aside the crushing, weighty belief that my hair in its natural state was wrong, an abomination, a transgression against natural law.

The 1968 assassination of Martin Luther King, Jr., unleashed fury in the Black community, and from the

ashen, smoldering pyres that filled so many Black neighborhoods destroyed and ruined in rebellions in the aftermath of King's murder rose the gospel of Black Power,
Black Consciousness, and Black Is Beautiful. It was as if we
had learned that the world was not round, it was really flat,
or that, no, White folks would not keep us down forever.
One day we would rule. Among the younger generation,
already seeking identity, the idea that Black was beautiful
became a kind of oxygen that we breathed. R&B king
James Brown even penned an anthem: "Say It Loud, I'm
Black and I'm Proud."

At American University where I was enrolled, majoring in English and American Studies, I was active in the
Black Student Union and wrote a weekly column for the
school newspaper about issues relevant to the Black community. Even there the unresolved issues around color and
identity and race raged.

The Black Panthers made regular forays onto campus to
recruit members from among the Black student population.
In their black leather jackets and black berets, with their
huge Afros and militant attitudes, the Panthers were irresistible to the Black girls on campus. But we soon realized
that most of the Panther brothers preferred White girls, or
as we bitterly and crudely joked, "white meat." In the new
Black studies courses that the university introduced, Black
psychology and Black sociology and Black history, we read
books that explained the pent-up anger of the Black male.
(What about the pent-up anger of the Black woman?) We
learned how anger, rage, and self-hatred led many Black

men like lemmings in the taboo-shattering period of the sixties to eagerly and often, and sometimes exclusively, develop a taste for the forbidden fruit of the White woman. It had nothing to do with the sisters, the books told us. The Black man was just working out his own psychosis. But as we sisters sat in the cafeteria or on the student commons watching the Panther brothers strutting across campus with a White girl on their arm, we felt it had a lot to do with us. And it wasn't just the Panthers. Brothers everywhere, it seemed, were jumping into bed with Miss Anne. The conclusion among many brown to black women was that now that a Black man felt free to go after a White woman, the "real" thing, the status and privilege of light-skinned Black women would be threatened.

But pretty soon the light-skinned, straight- and "good"-haired girls, who had in the face of the Afro despaired at the inability of their hair to kink up, learned and shared and traded the concoctions and the secret brews to give them the perfect high-riding Angela Davis 'fro. Then they had it all. Light skin and keen features (which were never truly dethroned by dark skin and full features, no matter how loudly we shouted "I'm Black and I'm Proud"), *and* they often had the biggest Afro in town.

Brown to black girls had a brief moment in the sun. We won a few beauty pageants, graced the pages of some of the major mainstream magazines. Brothers started calling us African queens and wrote poetry filled with militant, devoted protestations of love and loyalty (as long as we created a lot of little warriors to save the race). Even *Ebony* and *Jet* eased up on their deeply entrenched colorism and featured a few darker-skinned sisters with naturals on their pages. I felt for the first time in my life comfortable in my brown skin. By the late sixties, I knew that I would never feel the need to apologize to myself or anyone else for how I looked. I knew that the way in which I raised my children, the qualities I sought in a lover, or a husband, or even a date, would be influenced by this cataclysmic social change. I was a living, breathing example of how a social and cultural movement could actually change a person's life.

However, on the home front, my Afro and my new attitude exploded like a Molotov cocktail. Along with the rest of my generation, I took a word, *black,* which had up until then been our parents' curse of choice—for example, "You black bitch"; "You black son of a bitch"; "You black (anything you could think of)"—and instead turned it into my name. *Black* previously had been the weapon of mass destruction of curses among Negroes, as we called ourselves then. There was no stronger word to use to vilify, abuse, or revile someone. If you wanted to have the final word in an argument, lay on someone the ultimate insult, or push an altercation up to the point of no return, you simply spit out the word *black.*

But in the sixties, we forged, with battles and blood and shouts and screams, a new way to talk. Now we said the word *Black* tenderly, respectfully. *Black Woman. Black Man. Black People. Black Pride.* We said it defiantly. *Black Power.* We said it over and over again. *Umgowah Black Power. Black Power. Black Power.* My mother took to brooding when she was around me, staring at me, with my Afro and love beads, as though I were a stranger, as though I were surely no child that she had ever borne. My Afrocentric father agreed with my politics but hated my Afro because of the manner in which it symbolized my growing independence. He was not ready to let me go or grow up quite yet. The rest of my family made jokes and derided the anger and militance of the loud, arrogant Black youth featured every night, it seemed, on the evening news.

I was angry, and my parents and relatives were afraid. I was angry at my mother for her colorist warnings. At all the teachers I'd had who taught me from books that never showed my face. At White people and the world they seemed to dominate and control. I was angry, but inside I was fragile and wanted more than anything for my parents, my elders, and my family to embrace and accept the new me.

But they were afraid. Very afraid. It was as though by saying that Black was beautiful I had violated a law of nature. And in a way I had. We were turning the world and all its conventional assumptions upside down. At some point in our racial past we knew that in our blackness we were merely and gloriously human. In our blackness we

were children of God. In our blackness we were no more
and no less than anyone else. But slavery, peonage, lynch-
ings, and Jim Crow segregation had imposed the most
abiding and wrenching amnesia. For a long and quite
lonely time, I was an outsider in my family because I ad-
hered to the new gospel.

And yet because we never addressed or dared to talk
about the insidious ways in which colorism had divided
and conquered us, even while focusing on the sins of "The
Man" and "The System" and "White Racism," my generation squandered a precious, perfect moment that could
have allowed us to move from a theoretical assertion that
Black Is Beautiful, to the first necessary, halting acceptance that it really is beautiful *in fact*. That black skin possesses a radiance and a depth that is regal and stunning.
That full lips are just that, full lips. They are not water-
melon or banana lips or any of the racist stereotypes propagated and encouraged by the larger culture and even by
Black people. They are just lips! And that a broad nose is
a nose. A nose that fits our phenotype. White people's lips
don't speak pearls of wisdom because they are thin. They
are body parts. Anatomy. But the activists of my generation, for all of our considerable and laudable courage,
failed to divest these images of their cultural definitions.
Because then we would have had to look into our own
tattered souls and trembling hearts and see how little love
we possessed for ourselves. But until we fessed up to the
self-hatred rooted in colorism, we would always be held

hostage to it. The Black community was a huge dysfunctional family made up of thousands of dysfunctional families, most of whom were in deep denial about the persistence of the color complex even in the age of "Black Is Beautiful." Oh, if just saying it had made it so. And so in the sixties we rattled the bars on the cage. We saw the keys to the door. But we were content to remain inside.

But I marched to my own drummer and buried the little girl inside of me that had always stood hunched or folded in on herself, the little girl who could be silenced and squashed and beaten down because she thought what the world felt mattered. I buried her. I let her go with love. I decided that because she was me I had to love her. I swept out the cobweb-filled corner where she had always stood fretting and afraid. I then turned on the lights in my soul and invited the other little girl who had been waiting in the shadows to step forth and stand up straight, to stand up tall, where everybody could see her and where I would never lose sight of her. She was a *badd* little sister, and I reached out and held her hand and I decided I would never let it go.

It is within our families that we learn to support, encourage, believe in, or deny the color complex. My father's siblings were all like him: tall, big-boned, dark men and women. On the rare occasions that I was in the presence of all of my paternal aunts and uncles I remember feeling as if I was surrounded by a race of some genteel but powerful breed of people so secure in who they were that they found the racial confusion of most others a source of pity and amusement. My father's siblings talked about Malcolm X with pride, not the fear he instilled in my mother. They were men and women for whom racial pride was the gospel. My father's sisters and female cousins confidently wore red and brown and even yellow, colors my mother swore were simply not made for me. They seemed not to know that they were supposed to think themselves ugly because of their dark skin, wide hips, and full-featured faces. I could tell, in fact, that the thought had never occurred to them.

My maternal grandmother, Molly Reid, was a stern, no-nonsense woman who with her part-time-preacher husband raised my mother and three sons in Greensboro, North Carolina. The colorist attitudes that my mother brought north with her surely were incubated in her childhood home and supported by the tightly knit segregated community in which she was raised. My grandmother, like my father, was very dark, but Granny Reid (beloved by her neighbors on McConnell Road for her generosity) wore her darkness like a shroud, like a veil that she could not remove, like a punishment she felt that she deserved. Her husband, my grandfather John Reid, was a stern, often silent, morose man to whom I was always utterly afraid to speak.

My grandmother's parents had surely been slaves. She would have been born during Reconstruction, a period in the South when Blacks who dared to vote risked lynching and Black communities were both flourishing and under siege, a time when many Black men were virtually re-enslaved under a brutal system of peonage for even minor crimes. It was also a time when many colleges for Negroes were being established in the South and were attended in some cases exclusively by mulattoes. A time when Black men who were able to become educated often adopted the patriarchal attitudes and cultural values of the White middle class. And these men, the precursors of today's Black middle class, often wanted wives cast in the mold of the mates of White middle-class men. Because of their need for status, and their equation of Whiteness with beauty, a dark-skinned woman was neither desired nor desirable.

Against this backdrop, it would have been easy, natural, for my grandmother to raise her children on the gospel of White Is Right, White Is Might, and Light Is Right. If she thumbed through a *Harper's* or an *Atlantic* magazine of that time, my grandmother would have seen the most base caricatures of Negro women and men, portraying them as bug-eyed, big-lipped, and sometimes drawn as beasts with tails. For a people whose hearts and minds and souls had been not just damaged but sometimes destroyed by generations of enslavement, acceptance of this self-image would have made a perverse kind of sense. "Why else would I have been made or born a slave," the most wretched freedmen and freedwomen might have asked themselves, "if I was not God's forgotten child?" I can never know the words my grandmother spoke to my mother and my uncles about color, but if it is true that the apple doesn't fall too far from the tree, blackness was taboo. And I often wonder how old my mother was when she was first told *"Don't play in the sun."*

Washington, D.C., where I was born, grew up, and attended college, the city I left in the early seventies and returned to in the mid-eighties, has long been recognized as one of the most color-conscious cities in America. Washington is a city that was home in the years immediately after slavery to a burgeoning Black leadership class. These were African American men and women who composed a kind of mulatto aristocracy. They were the offspring of coercive or consensual unions between White men and enslaved or free Black women. They were the children of Black men and White women. They were Blacks through whose veins enough White blood had been passed down through the generations to encode "White" features, and they had benefited, as much as was possible under a brutal and stringent system of overt racism, segregation, and denial of rights, from the accident of their birth.

This mulatto elite ruled the Black social and political spheres in other cities, Philadelphia, Atlanta, Charleston, New York, and New Orleans among them. But Washington, D.C., became in the minds of many the "capital" of colorism. I grew up in the shadow of a colorist past that in-cluded "Blue Vein" societies in D.C., which would not allow membership to anyone whose veins could not be seen through the skin. In the early days of segregation in Washington, the children of D.C.'s light-skinned middle and upper classes attended the academically rigorous Dunbar High School, where they learned to think and become leaders. The dusky-hued sons and daughters of the lower class attended Armstrong, where they were trained to work with their hands.

I had little if any interaction with the light-skinned elite, but their codes of conduct, their etiquette, their colorist beliefs and practices, were well known in the Black community and for the most part when I was a child went unchallenged. Colorism existed like a bitter, unalterable pollutant in the atmosphere of the Black community, something of which we were all aware and yet tried to ignore.

I do not believe that the Black leadership class was more colorist than other Blacks. Listen closely to the lyrics of many blues songs, and to the self-hating colorism woven into our southern folklore, folk tales, and jokes. Colorism knows no class boundaries in the Black community. But the men and women of the Black leadership class developed more openly elaborate rituals, attitudes, and strategies to maintain lightness, White blood, and the status it conferred than other Blacks. And for all their education and refinement, color was a serious issue among these people, discussed often in the crudest terms. High-class, light-skinned mothers and fathers routinely warned their children not to "bring home any dark meat."

———

When I was a teenager in D.C. I never attended a cotillion, but I heard about them. I saw pictures in the *Washington Afro* of these lavish coming-out parties for the daughters of D.C.'s Black upper class. Reading the accounts of these social events, I was struck, even as a teenager, by the ostentatiousness of the displays and didn't understand why this particular ceremony was so important. But it *was* important, for it introduced these young women in a formal way to the men of their class, the young men who because of birth, family, status, skin color, achievement, would be suitable mates. And it confirmed that these young women, for the same reasons, were acceptable.

And in D.C. there was "The Gold Coast," where the upper-class Blacks lived. "The Gold Coast" was the vernacular for Sixteenth Street, which is the exact center, the meridian of the city, and which stops in its tracks at the door of the White House. Sixteenth Street is known for its expensive, one-of-a-kind homes. Black doctors, lawyers, senior government civil servants, all lived on Sixteenth Street. Not every Black person who lived on Sixteenth Street was light-skinned, but it sometimes seemed most of them were.

I attended Western High School in the mid-sixties, then one of the two remaining racially integrated schools in the city. The children of ambassadors, White House staff, Cabinet members, and Sixteenth Street families attended Western. I loved the racial and ethnic diversity of the school and thrived in its academically challenging and competitive atmosphere. Western was a school comprised largely of the privileged, where class, race, economic background, and color mattered. The cheerleaders were usually White or light-skinned Black girls. The Black girls who dominated the social life of the school were mostly light-skinned daughters of affluent families. Some of the Black girls started a kind of invitation-only social club at the school, and no girl whose parents were divorced could join.

In my junior year, the nearly White, green-eyed, blond Black daughter of a prominent family started dating a member of the football team, who was an ebony version of Denzel Washington. But when Melinda introduced Doug to her parents, her father told her she could not date him because he was too dark. Gossip about this incident spread quickly through the school grapevine. Although Melinda was willing to defy her parents, for Doug the snub was too much and he started dating someone else.

I sometimes felt like a sharecropper living on the fringes of a vast palatial plantation, staking out my claim on the worst "bottom land" at Western. I felt this way even though I ran (unsuccessfully) for an office in the student government and found a satisfying niche writing for the school newspaper. My brown skin, my Black features, my coarse hair, my economic background (by this time my parents had separated and my mother and I lived in a small apartment in a well-kept low-income housing project), my knowledge that I did not fit the profile of the girl most likely to . . . (succeed, be homecoming queen, etc., etc.), made me feel on too many days like Cinderella before she was transformed by her fairy godmother. I had a small group of friends, young men and women who were brown like me. We lacked the charisma, the money, and the charm to be social kings and queens. But we were smart, gave one another comfort and support, and loved much about the school, even as we were aware that Western could never really belong to us. I studied hard, made good grades, and didn't set my social aspirations too high. I wasn't Icarus, and my mother had already warned me about the sun.

Howard University, long a beacon in and builder of the Washington and national Black community, was known when I was an adolescent living not far from its campus for being a blatantly color-conscious environment. The school was known for sororities, fraternities, parties, and its color code. An administrator at Howard who graduated from the school in 1962 told me, "Back then color was an issue and everybody knew it. Among the sororities, for example, the AKAs and the Deltas ruled the campus. And I remember hearing people say awfully cruel things about the Zetas. They were called the black and ugly sorority because most of their members were brown-skinned or dark-skinned. And it wasn't until 1962 that we had a brown-skinned girl as homecoming queen."

Howard's colorist history was one of the reasons that I did not apply to the school. Colorism was in fact the reason that I chose to apply only to White colleges and universities. I knew that colorist attitudes were a reality at many historically Black colleges. I felt that I could handle racism at a White school more effectively than colorism at a Black school. Because the color complex is a form of intraracial genocide, because it positions Blacks versus Blacks, the emotional toll it imposes and the lack of trust or acceptance of others that it breeds are exhausting and demoralizing. I looked forward to college as a place where I could finally be *me*. I wasn't sure who I was, but I wanted to try to find out in an environment where maybe, just maybe, the color, if not the racial playing field, would be more level.

At a White school, I wouldn't have to worry about whether or not I was light enough to be the homecoming queen or to join the AKAs or date the head of student government. I knew that racism at a historically White college would impose social limitations. I would be interacting with Whites in a virtually all-White environment, an experience that was new and unexpected, and that little in my life had prepared me for. Yet I felt instinctively that on a White campus I would and could find a way to be my Black self the way I wanted to be. The sororities wouldn't be recruiting me, so they were irrelevant. I'd find a boyfriend back in the hood, not on campus. And I wasn't concerned about academics; that had always been my strong suit. There would be issues, no doubt, but I convinced myself that colorism wouldn't be one of them. I had been wounded, and quite deeply, by colorism in my eighteen years. Now that I was nearly an adult, I wanted to opt out of any situations that could rekindle pain that was never far from the surface.

Students are drawn to Howard because perhaps attending a historically Black college is a tradition in their family. For the ambitious, and the driven and career-conscious, Howard offers access to future Black leaders. My ambitions were academic and intellectual, not social. And for Black students who have grown up with little interaction with a large, sustaining Black community, Howard provides a chance to "connect" with Black folks. I had grown up among Black people from a host of lifestyles and life situations as a result of the boarders in my mother's houses. I had nothing in particular to prove or disprove by attending Howard.

With its intricate network of social expectations, its particular definitions of what was acceptable or permissible for educated Blacks, Howard loomed like a straitjacket. I wanted to rebel. I wanted to recast and remake myself. Howard did not seem to me to be the place where I could do that.

But ironically, the Black Power and Black Consciousness Movements that spread like seismic eruptions throughout the country changed much at Howard, including the most odious and blatant manifestations of the color complex. While I attended American University in upper-northwest Washington, I enrolled in a Swahili class offered at Howard and attended go-down-in-history-good parties on the campus. And, as we sat on the front steps of a brownstone not far from the campus one sultry June night, sipping sangría and listening to Gil Scott Heron and The Last Poets, a dashiki-clad Howard senior, just before his lips touched mine, called me an "ebony queen."

Silences and Secrets

The biggest misconception about the color complex among
people of African descent is that it is about beauty. The
color complex is about power, status, and privilege.

—DR. JAMILA KIZUWUNDU

I am asked to make a Black History Month appearance
at the high school where my husband, Joe, teaches.
During an hourlong session in the library, I read from
and discuss my writing with three classes of juniors and
seniors. The following day, one of the students who attended the program passed my husband in the hallway on
her way to a class. The young girl told him, "Mr. Murray, I
didn't know your wife would look like *that*." For this young
girl, my husband's choice of a brown-skinned mate has
confounded her expectations.

I am having dinner with a Famous Black Writer. Along
with three White female faculty members from the English department at a university where he will read later

that evening, I am sipping wine and enjoying the food in a pricey, cozy, and elegant French restaurant. The Famous Black Writer has won many awards for his novels about life in the South. I have taught his work in a number of African American literature classes. I admire the work of the Famous Black Writer, and teach him as an example of exemplary writing and powerful discourse. But I have long been disturbed by the portrayals of Black women in his work that lock them into roles of nurturer/mammy/faithful wives or seductive sirens. The Famous Black Writer portrays women through a colorist vision. Dark-skinned women are usually mammy/nurturers or asexual, domineering hags. Light-skinned women are objects of desire and sexual beings, understanding, faithful and true.

The Famous Black Writer spends much of the dinner openly assessing me. In vain I attempt small talk, but because he is used to being lionized, ingratiated, the center of attention, the Famous Black Writer greets my attempts at dialogue with barely disguised indifference. Yes, the Famous Black Writer is old enough to be my father. No, I do not know personally many of the other Black writers of his age that he asks me if I know during a gentle but insistent interrogation of my connections. But he is a Black writer and so am I. He is a Black man. I am a Black woman. I came to the dinner thinking that would count for something. The other women at the table attempt to facilitate conversation that includes me, but nothing works. By the time dessert arrives I am reeling with a sense of déjà vu as I recognize the kind of courtly contempt that I have sensed on other occasions, especially from older, colorist, class-conscious Blacks who, finding themselves in social situations with a short Afro–wearing, brown-skinned woman like me, can barely contain their disappointment that a woman of my achievements (as an author and professor) looks the way I do. The short hair. ("Why would a woman willingly wear her hair that short, when she probably doesn't have much to begin with?") The brown skin. The "Black" features. ("That can't be helped but still . . .") For these folks, Black success and achievement simply don't come wrapped in the package I present. And, conversely, I have found myself accepted in many cases by these same folks because my status as a published writer neutralized and "trumped" my "problematic" appearance. But the Famous Writer sits for most of the dinner furtively gazing at me now and then, wondering, I am sure, "How did you get in here?" And I sit through most of the dinner thinking about those dark-skinned women in his novels, fully convinced that he could never imagine himself breaking bread with them either.

I am in my late thirties, a divorced single mother, a professor, a writer. And, like almost all of my girlfriends, I am looking for love. We get together over dinner to spend Friday nights in the throes of "Sisterfriend" chat and gossip, and inevitably we talk about men. About *the Brothers*. We bemoan our good jobs, our money in the bank, our steady creep toward forty, or our single parenthood, wondering if these things (that we worked hard for, chose, or can't help) are repelling *the Brothers*. But even with my Sisterfriends I never share the secret fear I have that among the strikes against me in finding Mr. Right is my color. I feel it. I fear it. But I never ever say it. At least not out loud.

Writing about the color complex means thinking about the color complex, and the process becomes akin to breaking through a dense, evil encryption that masks, hides, denies, and silences the truth about what we have inflicted on ourselves. Writing this book, I surrender to memory. Writing this book, I inevitably seek out and find others brave enough to witness, question, and remember.

I am in graduate school in New York, and my roommate comes in one evening from dining with a male buddy. She is studying drama at New York University, and her friend wants to and eventually will become a playwright of some note. Wanda and I have been friends since high school. We are two brown girls who turned Black and Proud together and between whom there are mostly no secrets. Her friend Oscar is the light-skinned only son of a prominent and influential African American family from Atlanta. I have always found Oscar rather odd. He constantly affects a veneer of pseudointellectualism that appears to be vital for his self-image. I have also always felt that Oscar was convinced of his superiority to both Wanda and me on several scores, including family background, color, and class. But I have never told Wanda my feelings. *This* is the one secret between us.

On this evening, Wanda, looking absolutely stunned, returns to our cramped West Side apartment and sinks into the thrift-store sofa in the claustrophobically small living room. For nearly half an hour she refuses to tell me what's wrong. Finally, after she has made herself a cup of chamomile tea and taken a few sips she tells me, "Over moo goo gai pan and sweet and sour pork, Oscar told me tonight that he really liked me a lot, but that I was too dark for him to ever take home to his family as anything other than just a friend."

"How did the subject come up?" I ask, attempting to evidence a surprise I don't really feel. I'm not surprised, but I am mad as hell, already sympathizing with the pain I know Wanda feels.

"That's the thing. It just came out of nowhere," she exclaims with a confused shake of her African cloth–wrapped head. "One minute we're talking about a LeRoi Jones' play, and then the next thing I know he's informing me that he could never take me home to meet Mom and Dad. I've never been interested in him in that way, and I don't know why he told me that," she muses sullenly, trying, I can tell, as is her way, to tap down, dissolve, and dilute just how wretched she feels. Sipping the steaming, too hot tea, she gives up and places the mug on the wicker table stacked with copies of *Essence, Black World,* and *Black Scholar.*

"The bastard. I don't even want his yellow ass!" Wanda shouts, biting her lower lip and storming into her bedroom. Wanda and I both figure that Oscar probably hasn't had a date in a very long time. He's nerdy, self-conscious, and painfully shy at the very moments when confidence is most required. But he is light-skinned, and Oscar has subjected my best friend to the equivalent of a colorist drive-by incident all in the name of establishing, *just for the record,* that although he may not be getting any nooky now, once he finds the right girl, she won't look anything like Wanda.

Flash forward twenty years. My sixteen-year-old son, Michael, and I are grocery shopping, and as we walk through the food aisles, we are discussing, once again, the videos on Black Entertainment Television. I am deriding them as I often do as sexist and macho, yet find myself in the uncomfortable position of wondering aloud to my son why there are only light-skinned girls in those sexist, macho videos. This is a squishy, squirmy position for me to be in as a feminist and a progressive. This is before India.Arie, and before blond-wigged Lil' Kim. But I push aside my concerns about the sexual exploitation of women via the images in the videos and rhetorically ask Michael why the love interests in the videos for romantic ballads are always light and bright, why the woman desired for love or lust is Latina, Asian, light-skinned, long-haired, keen-featured, or any racial configuration except one that resembles his mama. I am not asking the questions for an answer but to make him think.

My first husband, Michael's father, is a dark-skinned Nigerian. Together we produced Michael, whose light tan complexion refutes my mother's genetic math. The African diasporic gene pool is tricky and unpredictable. Some Ethiopians and Egyptians look like Caucasians with a tan. I mated with a man as dark as my very black father and produced a son a shade lighter than me.

Michael is tall; he will eventually grow to be six foot three. His face is a nearly perfect amalgam of his father's and mine. Women friends often tell me how handsome Michael is, and that he looks like I "spit him out." As Michael's mother, I've never spent much time evaluating him on a scale of one to ten. My son possesses an easygoing, boyish charm. When I look at him objectively (can a mother ever pull that off?) I can see that he is attractive. But I am also aware that Michael's complexion, his somewhere in the middle, not too dark complexion, makes it easier for him to be seen as handsome.

Because of the colorist conflicts in my family, raising Michael I was hyperaware of the need to inculcate a sense of racial pride. I have talked honestly with him about the way that I was raised, tried to emulate my father's hands-on, direct approach to the passing down of African and African American history, even sending him at one point to an Afrocentric school. I also share with Michael the complexity of my mother's attitudes and try to explain with compassion and understanding the lessons she taught me about color.

Opening the freezer-section door and reaching for a box of Steak-Ums, Michael shrugs uneasily, and I sense loyalty to his adolescent tribe for whom the videos are anthems. My teenage heroes were Muhammad Ali, Martin Luther King, Jr., Malcolm X, Huey Newton, Angela Davis. My son's generation's heroes are Ice T, Ice Cube, and Tupac. But as we are standing in line at the checkout stand, Michael opens up, and with embarrassment and discomfort tells me about his friends' making fun of dark-skinned girls on the bus when he is coming home from school, of how his friends consider the word *black* a curse that they use to humiliate or tease the dark-skinned girls. "Mom, it's like 'black' is the worst thing you can call somebody." When Michael tells me this, I recall the attempts of my generation to rehabilitate the meanings of the word in our community. Then Michael tells me that his friends say they don't like dark-skinned girls because they have too much "attitude."

"Do you ever make colorist jokes?" I ask.

"*Maaaaa!*" he shouts, as though stung by the question.

"Do you?" I insist, perfectly comfortable conducting this grilling while standing in the middle of Safeway.

"Naw," he tells me. Over the next several years my son will date a number of girls, and I will notice that many of them have my complexion or are darker. Just as women often fall in love with men who evoke memories of their fathers, men often are drawn to women who remind them of Mama.

By the time Michael tells me all this we are removing vegetables and fruit, canned goods and paper products from the basket, placing the items on the conveyor belt. My anger and sense of outrage are congealing into a hot, thick bubble in the pit of my abdomen. But whom and what am I most angry with? Michael's friends, who are simply honoring a generations-old tradition of intraracial humiliation and degradation of the darkest among us? Their parents, who I suspect may not have talked to their children about the color complex? Everything the boys see around them that supports their denial of blackness, their willingness to be African American as long as they don't have to be too dark?

Enraged at the thought of the two-strikes law (black girls are dark *and* full of attitude) that Michael's friends impose on young women, I tell Michael as we unload the bagged groceries, placing them in the trunk of my car, "Dark-skinned Black girls had better have attitude. That's the only thing that saves them in a world that pretends they're not there or tries to erase them." I am at this point trembling with rage, whispering the words through clenched teeth, struggling not to go ballistic in the parking lot of Safeway.

Attitude. Years have passed since that conversation with my son, but I have probed and picked over the implications of that word, mulled over the charge, felt it like a lump of spoiled food I am expected to digest. Even now I can't seem to get that word out of my mind. *Attitude*. The word reminds me of how as a brown-skinned woman I always, even now as a middle-aged mother of an adult son, the author of several novels and works of nonfiction, a university professor, lecturer, and partner/friend/spouse to one of the best men in America, I still feel that I have to work harder to be seen, heard, valued, accepted, than if I were lighter-skinned.

I plead guilty to the charge. I do have attitude. Without it I would not have survived the scorn of my Black brothers and sisters or the racism of Whites. Yes, my hands are on my hips to ground and steady me in an unfathomable, unstable, and often unwelcoming society. In film and on television, brown to black women are so often portrayed as loud, angry, impatient, sometimes nearly crazed. And the darker they are, the louder, angrier, more impatient, and crazier they appear to be. These awful, stubborn stereotypes are inflicted on me relentlessly. But the stereotypes capture a bitter truth. Walk down a street in the hood, look inside an office on the thirty-third floor of a skyscraper, pull back the skin of our midnight dreams, and you will hear us. We are shouting. Screaming. Yelling for our psychic lives. Darker-skinned Black women know in their hearts and live with a terrible secret: Our men (our psychic twins, our alter egos) often don't value us as we are. As God has made us. And we scream, choking on our own guilty colorist rejection of our black/brown/dark-skinned brothers, whom we reject and are afraid to love because in their darkness we see the nothing, the void, the absence, that we fear is the sum total of what we are. For some of us there is more than a pinch of truth to the assertion that Black men and women fear and loathe one another even more than we fear and loathe the system of racism that imprisons us. And we know as well that we don't know how to love or value ourselves. Nobody will talk about this, so we fill the silence with a primal scream, a howl so deep and long and loud that it is the sound of life and the sound of death.

And yet all that attitude that we use as a psychological protective coating can backfire and ensnare us, catching us in its grip like a small animal in a trap. Darker-skinned women can sometimes turn rejection into a self-fulfilling prophecy. If a woman assumes she won't be heard, she will shout when perhaps she could whisper. If she fears she won't be loved, love will become impossible. If she fears she is not beautiful, she can never see her own worth in her eyes or the vision of anyone else. And the problem with too much attitude is that is separates us from others, it becomes a wall. No one cares that we stand trembling and hopeful beneath the anger on the other side. And *attitude* leads to mistrust and makes real intimacy difficult. How much of the color complex infects and influences the way that Black men and women love and attempt to love one another?

When I talked casually with a group of male seniors at the high school where my husband teaches math and computers, they admitted that relationships with light-skinned girls and what they generically called "black" girls were vastly different. They acknowledged that they saw beauty more easily in the lighter-skinned girls, that they felt darker-skinned girls were more vindictive when crossed or disappointed, lighter-skinned girls more sexually satisfying, darker-skinned girls more difficult to please. These young men, future husbands and fathers, had developed a complex philosophy about love and sex that was deeply influenced by perceptions of, prejudices about, and the impact of the color complex.

Bossy. Domineering. Hard. Bitchy. Difficult. These words are so often used to describe the "black black" woman and her brown-skinned sisters. And sometimes the charges are rooted in as much truth as stereotype. Do we become our stereotype? And yet these women, these "black black" and dark brown women often feel that they have less power and less control over their lives, receive less respect, and are valued and loved less. And in order to feel in control, in order to impose balance in the face of chaos, they exert control, they take over situations, they speak up often and loudly. In the past they were called "Sapphires" after the wife of the character Kingfish on *The Amos 'n' Andy Show.* Today they are called "Sheniquas," the all-purpose name for the embarrassing ghetto girl who snaps her fingers and twists her neck and whose hands are glued to her hips. Without these qualities few Black women could survive being Black and female, life in the hood, single motherhood, or even in some cases the battle zone of corporate America. The problem is that we laugh at these images, and yet they reflect the ease with which strength and determination when marshaled by darker-skinned women become a source of discomfort, a reason to inflict emotional abuse in the guise of humor and marginalize women in the Black community who are not considered dark and lovely but rather dark and ugly.

At the local post office, one of my neighbors whom I have not seen in several weeks asks about Joe and Michael and if I am writing any new books. Janet is a poised, delicately beautiful woman who manages to always look elegant, even on this day, wearing jeans and a bulky turtleneck sweater. We catch up on family, and when I tell her about this project she says, "Girl, we need to talk about that." Her husband owns a software company that is one of the most successful Black-owned businesses in the county in which we live. Janet is a senior administrator with a federal government agency. Their children attend one of Washington's premier private schools. "Has the color complex been a problem for you?" I ask as we stroll toward our cars, parked side by side, mine a Toyota, hers a BMW. Opening the car door and tossing her shoulder bag into the car, Janet turns to me and asks, "Didn't I ever tell you? When Wendell and I go to parties, sometimes people are shocked to see me with him. They obviously expected him to marry a sister with a different look. They think I'm too dark for him, because of what he's accomplished. He's even been asked why he married me." No, Janet had never told me this before. We are neighbor-friendly, going to dinner every few weeks with two other couples who live in our suburban community. I had never suspected that her marriage to Wendell, a wisecracking, Brooklyn-born wheeler-dealer two shades lighter than Janet's dark-hued, lovely complexion, would be embroiled in color politics. Janet has always struck me as assured and confident. She is, but the shrug and the pursed-lip smirk that follows her revelation are, I am certain, hard-won.

A friend who knows I am writing this book calls me one evening, upset because her son was told by an older female cousin "not to ever bring any black girls home." She wants to know how to handle the situation. She is as concerned about the effect of the admonition on her son as she is about what the words reveal about the emotional well-being of the overweight, full-featured, ebony-hued female cousin who gave her son this warning.

My husband Joe is a cancer survivor. After undergoing eight months of radiation and chemotherapy, he returned to work. The chemotherapy treatments altered his cell structure and changed the texture of his hair, making it straight rather than coarse. On his first day back at school one of his female colleagues welcomed him back and then looked closely at him and said, "You look great now. I see the cancer gave you good hair."

A young woman whom I am mentoring in a creative writing class submits a story about three young girls who go to a nightclub on a Saturday night. In the story the heroine is told by a young man as they are dancing, "Dang, you're cute for a dark girl." When I ask Kim about that comment she tells me simply, "That happened to me."

A few weeks after I see Janet at the post office, we finally talk. Sitting in her tastefully decorated living room, we are surrounded by walls filled with tie-dyed swaths of cloth from the Ivory Coast and Senegal, a silkscreen by a Haitian artist, and a carving of a Black Madonna. The hardwood floors shimmer, and the room manages to be both cozy and elegant. Janet's two children, Imani and James, have been sent upstairs, and we have the first floor of her five-bedroom house to ourselves.

When I ask Janet to talk to me about how the color complex has played out in her life, she turns thoughtful and then says, "Well, in Wendell's family there was an issue over my color. His mother thought that I was too dark for their family. I found this really strange, because, as in most Black families, skin tones ran the whole gamut with them. Wendell is a couple of shades lighter than me, but he has brothers and sisters who are darker than he is."

"How did you find out about his mother's feelings?"

"He told me."

"What was your reaction?"

"By that time in my life I was at a point where I knew that she had the problem, not me."

"Clearly Wendell likes a little 'brown sugar,' " I tease Janet.

"That's true, but it wasn't always that way. In college he dated a very light-skinned girl for several years, and the whole family expected him to marry her. So I guess it was a shock when he brought me home in what was considered her place."

"What happened with them?"

"It's really interesting. He told me that he got tired of dating light-skinned girls. He said that they seemed so caught up in the hype about them. He felt like the girl he was dating had lost a sense of who she was. He said he felt that darker-skinned sisters were more real."

"More real?"

"It's a difficult situation. I feel for light-skinned women sometimes in that they get it from all sides. On the one hand everyone wants them, but on the other hand they're sometimes told they aren't black enough to be the real thing, in terms of blackness. And then sometimes they *do* get pumped up, filled with a sense of superiority."

"Damned if they do . . ."

"Right."

"How was it for you in your family?"

"There were five of us, and once again we were a kind of rainbow of shades within the brown to black spectrum. But I was the middle child and I was the darkest child. Sometimes as a family we weren't really aware of the color issue until someone outside the family made a remark."

"Such as?"

"Oh, like if I was with my friends and my sister Karen, who was always considered the cutest and who was the lightest one of us, came around, and I introduced her as my sister. There'd sometimes be a reaction like, 'She's *your* sister?' You know, disbelief, or sometimes my status would rise. And it always seemed that my sisters and brothers always had the most popular friends, and when my parents gave us gifts they somehow got the nicest presents. I don't know how much of this had to do with my being a middle child and getting lost in the shuffle, but I know that some of it was about color too."

"How did this affect you?" I ask.

Up until this point in our conversation Janet has been poised, relaxed, and calm, but suddenly I can sense her tense up. I am maybe eight feet away from her, sitting in a leather recliner, and I watch her shift in agitation on the sofa. She folds her arms across her chest and looks away from me, purses her lips, and is silent for several moments before she speaks.

"I know it affected me. And I've actually thought about this quite a lot. I know that the reason I worked so hard to be smart in school and to achieve all that I have is related to being dark-skinned. I always felt like more was expected of me and that I had more to prove and that since that was the way things were I would be the best, the absolute best, at whatever I did."

Her voice quivers with a quiet, firm determination and a sublimated rage that I know all too well. She is gently pounding one fist in the palm of her other hand as she makes her point. "I was the one who graduated summa cum laude, the one who got a graduate degree. And even though we don't openly deal with it, when my brothers and sisters come to visit Wendell and me, I can feel this undercurrent of surprise and resentment that I am the one, the middle child, the darkest child, who outstripped them all. Wendell has been written about in the papers, has gotten awards for his business success. My brothers and sisters have jobs. I have a career. Wendell and I are doing better not just in our material lives but in our spiritual lives than my brothers and sisters, and I can almost hear my siblings asking themselves every time they come to visit us 'How did *she* do so well?' And probably thinking, 'Everything she's got is supposed to belong to me.' "

I share with Janet my own deeply embedded awareness of a double standard that asked and required more of me because of my color. We share anecdotes and incidents that testify to the resilience and grit we have developed over the years. Janet mentions that she is a member of the AKA sorority and says, "Even among my sorors, I find that when a light-skinned sister is not doing so well, when she's facing the kinds of disappointments that we all are bound to face, there's sometimes this sense that she has been cheated, denied in a way that is deeper and more painful than for women who don't look like her."

"So you're an AKA? I thought that was the sorority famous for the paper bag test?"

Janet laughs, and I am glad to see her release some of the tension that has built up. "Oh, those days are long gone. That was mostly in the South that the color thing was a big factor. My mother was an AKA."

"How does color play out among your sorors?"

"A while back there was an incident that, when I think about it now, I am pretty ashamed of. There was a group of us brown-skinned sorors who used to get together for what we called 'sistergirl evenings.' We would rent a movie, do a potluck dinner, and just chill at one of our houses, gossip, catch up on things, and relax. But there was one soror that we never invited. She was very light-skinned, had the hair and the features, the whole thing, and she had come from a pretty affluent, well-connected family. To us she didn't 'get down' or 'get Black' quite enough for us to feel comfortable including her in our gatherings. Well, finally after a while she confronted us about this and told us that she was deeply hurt and felt that we were discriminating against her. She forced us to confront the fact that we were indeed insecure, uptight, around her and that we had hurt her pretty badly."

"What happened?"

"As a group we had several conversations with her that were very, very honest. She got to confide how insecure she had felt around us and how our exclusion had fed into feelings she had from a childhood of having to prove her Blackness. In the end, after we talked openly and honestly, we invited her to the evenings and she fit right in."

I left Janet's house that evening filled with a sense of how the color complex spreads like a stain over so much of what we think and do. It intersects with issues of class and background, alters friendships, and turns its victims into victimizers. My conversation with Janet forces me to re-member a meeting with a grants officer at a local charity I had the week before. The executive is African American, friendly, genial, and has pledged support for a foundation that I head that supports Black writers. In his office on the top floor of a downtown D.C. office building, after we dis-cuss the grant he has secured for the foundation, we talk about our college days, our childhoods. Because he is light-skinned and comes from an upwardly mobile, striving family that includes a scientist brother at NIH and a psy-chologist sister (all this comes out as we chat), as I listen to his easy, humorous anecdotes about growing up in Germantown in Philadelphia, I am also judging him, put-ting him in a box in my mind. All because he is light-skinned. I am sure that I know what his wife looks like. I am convinced that I know what his friends look like. He has secured a major grant for my foundation, and I sit jok-ing and laughing with him, yet smugly assuming that for all his easy wit and despite how comfortable he makes me feel, that in his world, his private world, all the people who matter to him look like him. I have scaled the colorist walls that have been thrown up in my path. But like every-one else, I am a child and a victim of the color complex. I build walls too.

In the days after my conversation with Janet I am hyperaware of colorist nuances and guilt-ridden because of the memory of my own colorist sins. I am seeing and hear-ing with a kind of radioactivity that makes words and ges-tures crackle with fully revealed intent. A close friend and I go out to dinner with others and as he is sharing an an-ecdote about his family he refers to himself as "little *black* me." My friend is very dark, and he has spoken with me of-ten of growing up in Virginia, where his grandparents greeted him when he came to visit them with the stern, grieving question "And whose little *black* child are you?" My friend has told me how the question distanced him from his grandparents, and how in those words he heard the rejection and denial of blackness. And yet he sits, telling a joke about his childhood and referring to himself in the language that is for him and for me and for us all a kind of native tongue. I build the same walls I try to tear down. And some part of my friend will always be "little *black* me."

Paul grew up in New Orleans and works as an editor for a New York City–based university press. While I am in New York to see a revival of Arthur Miller's *The Crucible*, Paul and I get together for dinner before the play. We talk

about film and old friends, politics, and a new book by a
Black feminist critic he is editing. And of course we talk
about this project.

"Good luck," he says, pushing aside a half-finished
plate of shrimp scampi as though just the thought of the
subject of the color complex has suddenly made his appetite vanish. "You know it's one of those things that I
guess we act on all the time but don't really like to think
about. I know in my family, I was pretty blind to how it
played out with us until one of my cousins mentioned some
things that I didn't see."

"Like what?"

"My mother's relationship with my sister, for example.
My mother was the only brown-skinned child in a family
of five daughters." Before Paul says another word, these
words alone prick me, touch a vulnerability buried deep
within me that lives also on the surface of all my memories
and my hopes. *The only brown-skinned child in a family of
five daughters.* I know instinctively what his mother must
have felt, feared, and dreamed.

"And now that I look back on my childhood I can see
that my mother clearly must have had some issues around
that," Paul goes on, reaching for his half-eaten roll and
smearing it with a film of butter.

"My cousins used to point out the condescending way
their mothers would talk to my mother, and the closeness
that their mothers had that my mother seemed to be ex-
cluded from. She grew up as the only dark girl among five

daughters and was sent along with her sisters to a Catholic school in New Orleans where she was outnumbered there by lighter-skinned Black kids."

Paul sits chewing his roll slowly and methodically, and I can tell that he is thinking about what he has just said, fretting about its implications but still willing to go further.

"And I found out that when she was a kid there was a family that lived in her family's neighborhood that she was very close to. They were very light-skinned, and the family lore has it that my mother sort of hung around them like a mascot. She was treated pretty badly by them. Because it was New Orleans and because of the family dynamics that I began to see after talking with my cousins, I'm pretty sure that my mother's siblings got something that she didn't get from her parents. I can say without a doubt now that my mother had 'issues.'

"And it was my cousins who made me really see the tensions between my sister and my mother. In our family there were two brown-skinned sons and one light-skinned daughter, my sister, who was not only light-skinned but who had what we used to call 'good hair.' Now the really odd thing is that my sister grew up without any sense of entitlement because she was light-skinned. She never, ever traded on being light. But my sister has often told me that when we were kids, she hated the way our mother would fawn over her, how she'd spend hours combing and touching my sister's hair, how she'd dress her up in frilly, lacy dresses and make her sit like she was on display for the family to see. And yet as my sister got older my mother was so critical of her. My sister felt that she could never do anything to please or satisfy my mother. They argued constantly. Thinking about it now, I think that as my sister changed from my mother's little girl to a young woman with her own sexuality, my mother saw her as a threat. This is all pretty weird as I hear myself telling you this, but I guess the weirdest part is that I really wasn't aware of my mother's behavior as symptomatic of some pretty deep wounds. Not until my cousins started talking about it with me.

"What I'm saying is that my mother was actually jealous of her daughter's looks. She envied her skin and her features. And she couldn't decide whether to put my sister on a pedestal or to punish her for how my sister reminded her that *she* wasn't light and bright.

"We never, ever had what you would call a healthy conversation about color in my family, not with my parents. There were jokes, and anecdotes and stories about family members who tried to pass for Creole and even to this day won't speak to my mother or father on the streets of New Orleans. But an actual conversation about colorism, what it was and how it hurt or how to deal with it? Never. I remember when I was in high school, taking a girl to the homecoming dance. She was a friend who I'd grown up with, and she was dark-skinned and I had always thought she was so pretty. I put her picture on my bedroom wall, and when my friends came over all of them teased me because they said she was too dark for me to date. I remember feeling really hurt by what they said."

"Why did you feel hurt?" I ask Paul.

"Because I guess I could maybe by osmosis feel the pain and rejection they were aiming at my friend. They had made that girl and me an outsider. It hurt too because when they said that to me I knew something about those boys, something I hadn't really known. And I guess it hurt because I wasn't sure that I'd ever be friends with them the way I had been before."

Imitation of Life; or,
The Revolution Will Not
Be Televised

A dark black actress was considered for no role but that of a
mammy or an Aunt Jemima. On the other hand, the
part-black woman, the light skinned Negress, was
given a chance at lead parts and was graced with a
modicum of sex appeal. The desirable black women
who appeared afterwards in movies often were the
"cinnamon-colored gals" with Caucasian features.
The mulatto came closest to the white ideal.

. . . .

Mammy is representative of the all-black woman,
overweight, middle-aged and so dark, so thoroughly black
that it is preposterous ever to suggest that she be a
sex object. Instead she was desexed.

—FROM TOMS, COONS, MULATTOES, MAMMIES AND
BUCKS: AN INTERPRETATIVE HISTORY OF BLACKS
IN AMERICAN FILMS BY DONALD BOGLE

Sapphire is on the warpath. In full-throttle "Sapphire" mode, she stands berating her husband, King Fish, for another ill-advised scheme gone awry. Head bowed, broad-brimmed trademark hat in hand, King Fish accepts the icy tongue-lashing but will eventually rise up and speak his defense, offering up a combination of hurt pride and a steady stream of malapropisms that define his buffoonish character. One hand stationed on an ample hip, the index finger of the other hand wagging like a motorized piston at King Fish's lowered bald pate, the features on her brown-skinned face twisted in a display of disgust, Sapphire is swiveling her head from side to side, her voice locked somewhere between a screech and a scream.

Did Sapphire teach me how to put my hands on my hips? How to stand implacable as an ebony Amazon before the object of my displeasure, my rage swirling like a force field, anguished, angry words tossed like a grenade?

From 1951 to 1966, when *Amos 'n' Andy* was taken out of syndication, the weekly comedy was one of the most popular shows on television. A reprise of the radio phenomenon, which was originally performed by two White actors, the show revolved around the escapades of George "King Fish" Stevens, his friends Amos and Andy, King Fish's wife, Sapphire, her mother, known as "Sapphire's Mama," and a slow-witted janitor named Lightnin'. The broad humor, which relied on Black stereotypes, made the show a ratings success but was so controversial that the NAACP called for its removal from the air.

As a child, nearly every day after school I sat in front

of our black-and-white floor-model Zenith television and watched the show. I laughed out loud at the outrageous characters and situations, even as I recognized them from Black folk humor. King Fish was a trickster, a blow-hard, a hustler, and a braggart. Sapphire was the voice of reason, as well as the ultimate bossy, dominating shrew.

In the realm of Black popular culture Sapphire came to represent all outspoken, take-no-prisoners and no-mess Black women. I remember hearing men call women "a Sapphire" in barely disguised tones of contempt. Sapphire was a weekly, sometimes daily guest in my home via the television screen. But she was much more than that. In the early to mid-1950s, Sapphire was the reigning and most frequent symbol of the brown to black African American woman on TV. Sapphire was funny, imposing, off-putting, too much to handle. There was nothing soft or lovable about Sapphire. She was brown-skinned, big-mouthed, and loud. And in some backwoods region of my mind, I am sure, Sapphire was who I was afraid I was. Who I was afraid I would grow up to be. I am sure that when I was a little brown girl I was afraid that the light/bright boys I hungered after didn't see me but saw Sapphire instead.

Sitting before the screen, eating an after-school snack of milk and cookies, I was laughing at the antics, the bluster, and the conflicts on the screen. Only now, having broken the seal on the box in my mind where I stored a lifetime's worth of colorist wounds, can I ask myself if my brown skin destined me to be a Sapphire too. I lacked the consciousness and the awareness then to articulate such blasphemy, but it did not seem, from what television told me, that there was any alternative. Sapphire reinforced everything I knew about what the world expected of and how the world perceived brown to black women. Was there a part of me that felt that if I didn't grow up to be Sapphire then I'd grow up to be Beulah, the fat, dowdy maid who kept order, restored calm, solved problems, and cooked and cleaned each week in the home of the White family she worked for? Sapphire became a symbol of the dark Black woman as control freak. Beulah was the Black woman as mammy.

I had watched some of the finest Black actresses in the country, Ethel Waters, Hattie McDaniel (who was the first Black woman to win an Oscar), and Louise Beavers play the role of Beulah. I knew that most of the brown to black women on television and in the movies were maids. I knew what that meant but was surely too terrified, as a child, to think too long about it. Who in my world would tell me that what I saw on television was "make-believe," "fantasy"; who in my world loved me enough to lie to me about that?

I was brown. Like Sapphire. Like Beulah. My color seemed to doom me to be either a nurturer or a nag. What I saw on TV was no more criminal than what I had been told or endured because of my brown skin. Does a little brown girl grow up to become "Sapphire" or her present-day incarnation, "Sheneneh," because color, like some twisted form of determinism, neutralizes any other identity? Can you be what you never see?

And then there was Cicely. Cicely Tyson, the first Black woman to wear her hair natural, in 1959, a full decade before the style became widely fashionable and acceptable. I was thirteen years old when I saw her for the first time, in 1963, on the gritty drama *East Side/West Side*, which starred George C. Scott as a New York City social worker dealing each week with the impact of a plethora of social ills on the lives of his clients. Cicely Tyson played a young social worker in his office named Jane Foster.

I had never seen a woman like Tyson on television or in film. Her dark skin was radiant, her face chiseled it seemed to me by the hands of some great cosmic artist. The eyes did not gaze, but plunged into the depths of what they saw. Oh, and the wide mouth through which she enunciated so clearly and passionately, the high cheekbones that bloomed so suddenly when she smiled or laughed. I remember wondering if a woman like this, inhabiting the few scenes she was in with an expansive yet elegant and somehow muted dignity, actually lived among ordinary Negroes. Could it be that she was indeed a child of a community still ill at ease with a beauty like hers? A beauty that was so breathtaking, so awesome, and *so black*?

Literally every time I saw Cicely Tyson act, I stripped another layer of skin from the tough husk of stereotype and convention that nailed me to an invisible but rough-hewn cross. I didn't have to be Sapphire or Beulah. I could be a queen. Because that is how Tyson laid claim to each moment on celluloid.

When Cicely Tyson gazed with absolute trust into the

eyes of her sharecropper husband, played by Paul Winfield, in the movie *Sounder*, I knew that a black Black woman could love and be the beloved of an honorable Black man.

Sapphire, Beulah, and the women whom Tyson made real were not easily forgotten, fictional types. They were women with whom I developed subliminal, sometimes confusing, long-term emotional relationships. Even when I tried to resist, I found myself influenced by Sapphire's anger (an echo of the anger that seeps genetically from generation to generation through the womb of Black mother to Black daughter) and Beulah's nurturing (Why do Black men call the women they love "Mama," if not because we can't stop loving them like they are children instead of men?); Tyson's complex characters were haunting and seduced my loyalty. They made me feel like the incarnation of Coltrane's "Alabama," Picasso's *Guernica*, Gwendolyn Brooks's "We Real Cool"—so deceptive and so river-wide, mountain-high that I will never know myself fully, even if I live a hundred years. And when Cicely Tyson married the ebony prince Miles Davis, they seemed to symbolize the ultimate in *Black love*. I grew up with these brown to black Black women as symbols, as metaphors that echoed or contradicted my mother's unforgettable admonition not to play in the sun.

But say Cicely Tyson's name today and for most Black baby boomers, several television shows are likely to spring to mind: *The Autobiography of Miss Jane Pittman*, for which Tyson won an Emmy; *Roots*, in which she was part of an all-star cast; *A Woman Called Moses* (a project she initiated on the life of Harriet Tubman); and most recently *Mama Flora's Family*. Say Cicely Tyson's name today and it often and unfortunately evokes responses like the one of a friend who said, "Oh, please, all those head-rag-wearing, long-suffering mammy roles she played—let's not even go there."

Still, as an actress, Cicely Tyson offered me as a brown woman an elevated and transcendent vision of myself. It was a vision that was useful because it was so honest. Like all great actresses, in one role Tyson could manifest the entire spectrum of human emotion and liberate her audience as they feasted on her performance as if it were the bread of life.

Like many of the finest Black actors, Cicely Tyson was never accorded her rightful place in the Hollywood firmament. She has become best known for roles that fit into the asexual heroic/valorous mold, because as a Black actress she was stereotyped. As a Black actress, she was not offered high-profile Hollywood career-making roles. As a Black actress she was undervalued. Yet Tyson acted gloriously in the roles that she could get and changed the system as much as she could. Playing Harriet Tubman in *A Woman Called Moses*, Tyson was nothing short of magnificent. Watching the TV movie I was amazed at the ways in which she made this iconic figure, shrouded in myth and legend, a living, breathing woman. A woman who was gifted and burdened with powerful visions, who fell in love with a man with whom she tried to live as wife and mate and friend, and who risked everything to save her people.

Cicely Tyson was not merely acting when she played the role of Tubman. She was channeling the soul and the spirit of a black African American woman. Honoring Tubman, Tyson honored herself. She honored all women of conviction and courage. And she gave a voice to all the women who looked like Harriet Tubman, women considered unfeminine because of their dark skin, their calloused hands, and their brave hearts. And as I had felt so often when watching Cicely Tyson at work, I felt that she was honoring me. *Finally, someone was honoring me.*

Cicely Tyson's magnificent women made inroads, but Sapphire and Beulah remained as ghosts. I carried them as invisible cargo, and I sometimes carry them still. In the fall of 1991 when NBC debuted the drama *I'll Fly Away*, all my Beulah-stuff, all my Black maid psychosis noisily awoke from what I had hoped was a permanent slumber.

The box office and critical success of the 1989 film *Driving Miss Daisy*, a nostalgic homage to the relationship between a grouchy elderly southern White woman and her Black chauffeur made the world suddenly safe in 1991 for a television drama about a Black maid working in the home of a prosecuting attorney in the South, set against the backdrop of the rise of the Civil Rights Movement.

I'll Fly Away brought forth all my memories of dark-skinned Black actresses playing servants, and for several weeks as a form of protest I resolutely refused to watch the program. And then friends began telling me that this Black maid was no Beulah. I gave in and watched the program and found over the course of the two seasons that the program aired that Lilly, played by Regina Taylor, had a complex, intricate emotional life and a family of her own that she did not sacrifice to care for her White charges. She was vulnerable and intelligent, and she had ambitions and a lover, and she asserted and protected her dignity and self-worth. She wasn't just a maid. She was a woman whom any woman, any person anywhere, could identify with and root for. She was a maid who instilled me with pride.

Regina Taylor, dark like Cicely Tyson and possessed of the same solemn dignity, allowed me to make peace with my memories of Beulah and Sapphire. Beulah and Sapphire, because they were such deeply ingrained stereotypes, were an important part of my cultural legacy. Watching Sapphire lay into King Fish or Beulah keep her White folks happy, I learned painful, difficult lessons about the status, the value, and the role of the brown to black women in the cultural imagination of America.

Week after week watching Regina Taylor's Lilly, however, I confronted what the stereotype of the Black maid and the strong dark woman was not intended to reveal, what it was designed to camouflage—the ways in which actual Black women who looked like Beulah and Sapphire had swallowed their pride while working in a White home or loving a weak Black man. What I could not see in the stereotype was the competence and creativity with which these women in real life and in these films "ran" the domestic sphere that was their domain. And of course the stereotype stripped these women, just as they were stripped in real life, of a way to speak eloquently about their pain, their desires, and their dreams and actually have someone listen. We heard Sapphire, but we never really knew her. Beulah wore a mask that hid her authentic Black self in the presence of "her White folks." But Lilly managed to make herself heard. By her emotionally distant father. By her White liberal employer. By her young daughter, to whom she promised the world. And in the final episode, which revisited the characters years later, she was making herself heard through the act of writing.

I'll Fly Away, a show I swore I would never watch, allowed me to lay down a good portion of my Beulah and Sapphire burden. This is why television matters, because it reflects us at our best and at our worst. I watch television a lot, even as I am always engaged in a tangled and intense tango of love and hate with the medium. Television has been and still is one of the culture's most powerful tools for spreading the gospel of the supremacy of whiteness. And I am always looking for me, *brown-skinned, coarse-haired me,* on the screen (as the sexy, strong-willed yet vulnerable female doctor; as the love interest of the handsome Black or White lawyer; even as the woman in distress the hero risks all to save). I look for me every time I turn on my set.

A screenwriter friend, who has written for a number of major Black and White prime-time network and cable dramas, and I chat about this book, and I tell him that I'd like to talk to somebody in the business about colorism as a factor in television casting. He makes a few calls, and

one afternoon I am talking long-distance to an African
American television producer. The producer agrees to talk
with me about colorism in television only if his name is
not used. The subject is too sensitive, too loaded, too
much a part of the business for him to risk attribution.

We begin by talking about racism in the film and television industry. He is bitter but determined to stay in the
field even as he acknowledges, "Right now there are only
three of *us* producing and it takes us much longer to move
up the ladder than other folks." He shares stories that il-
lustrate the racist, clubby, inbred nature of the industry
which he says is still "White boy run although we're here
for window dressing." We talk about his experience at
several different networks, the politics of just getting a
"Black" show on the air, and the contradictory response of
the Black community to quality Black shows. "Our folks
only support the serious, groundbreaking shows once
they're canceled," he says. "We never write any letters of
praise before they get cut. The NAACP is nowhere to be
found to praise the networks for airing a show that is a risk,
only around to turn on the heat when it's canceled." We
are talking about racism, and he is clearly comfortable with
this dialogue, even though it depends on his admitting
that in his chosen career he has influence but no power
and that his frustrations are frequent and mighty. Within
minutes of beginning our conversation, I realize that we
will have to circle around the topic at hand, back into it.
It is a subject that he has agreed to discuss but that I will
have to force him to dive into. Yet I am grateful that he

agreed to talk to me at all, for my screenwriter friend told me that absolutely none of the White male executives who decide which shows get on the air and which ones do not were willing to be interviewed on this subject.

When we finally begin talking about the dynamics of the color complex in casting, the producer begins by saying, "Beauty plays a great role in casting. Most actors cast on television shows are exceptionally attractive. Most of TV is really an excuse to provide eye candy for the viewers."

I am hearing this and wondering if this is his excuse for the industry's colorist practices. That is, brown to black women aren't exceptionally attractive, ergo their absence from or marginalization in TV ads and shows.

"I'm not gonna let you off that easy." I laugh and then say, "You know what I see when I look at television? Dark-skinned Black men on the six o'clock news wanted for murder or mayhem. Dark-skinned gangsta thugs in music videos. Erudite, light-skinned Black men and keen-featured light-skinned women reading the news on CNN and MSNBC or as anchors on the evening news shows and the morning news/talk shows. I see that almost all the Black actors on my favorite soap opera, *The Young and the Restless,* are light. I see brown to black women telling you how to clean your kitchen floor or your toilet bowl or get rid of constipation. While 'Sarah' is cleaning the bathroom or mopping the kitchen floor on TV, her light-skinned sister, who may be 'ethnically ambiguous,' is romping it up with her White pals, on the beach, drinking upscale coffee in a chic café, making dinner with her White buddies while comparing the benefits of a particular brand of the Pill, or grooving in the backseat of a Mazda to jazz or rap while snuggled up beside a young White boy. Clearly the light, bright sister 'belongs.' I see all that and the message I get is that from the kitchen, or the back room, the darker-skinned Blacks are making the Big House of America a clean, safe place for the lighter-skinned Blacks to live in *with* the good White folk. And I see Halle Berry given a kind of 'honorary White' status because of her biracial beauty." When my rant is finished, the producer laughs as though relieved by my frankness. Then we get down to business. Still we play a verbal game of cat and mouse as he remains a reluctant informant, but the producer does acknowledge some points:

"Both Black and White directors cast according to European concepts of beauty."

"You will see dark-skinned women cast on television when it's an agenda item, when the show wants to be *realistic*. Like a cop show or a program that deals with the inner city. But if it's a show where the beauty of the Black female character is important, where she has to be eye candy, you are more likely to see light and bright than dark and lovely."

"There are arguments all the time in casting sessions about Black actresses and whether they are pretty enough to meet White standards."

I share with the producer a conversation I had with a Black woman journalist who has written extensively about the industry. She told me about what Black casting directors call "The Mulatto Follies," a situation where darker-skinned actresses don't even show up in response to a casting call. I tell the producer that this journalist asked me rhetorically, "Who knows what a darker-skinned actress has gone through to get to a point where she gets cast in a major role? Acting is a really rough-and-tumble, cut-throat business for everybody, with audition after audition and cut after cut. Darker-skinned actresses are less likely to believe they are attractive and maybe simply don't have the thick skin required to get rejected and wonder if it's about color rather than their talent."

The producer says he has heard the phrase and seen the phenomenon of "The Mulatto Follies," but he assures me that Black directors are aware of the issue and cites White producers like David E. Kelley who regularly cast darker-skinned African American actors in lead roles.

I ask him why there appear to be more darker-skinned Black women in lead roles in serious dramas on cable.

"They are willing to take risks in casting that the networks aren't," he says.

But what sticks in my mind as we continue to talk is that the producer has confirmed what television tells me every time I turn it on: Darker-skinned Black women with identifiably "Black" features are not deemed attractive and so are inevitably cast as domestics (*I'll Fly Away*), harried manic-depressive public school teachers (*Boston Public*), no-nonsense, capable defense attorneys (*The Practice*). It's news to me that the sisters in these programs are not attractive! I am glad the sisters are getting a payday. Thankful that these fine actresses are employed! I'm just waiting to turn on my screen one day and see them cast *against* the dominant, aggressive, got-all-the-answers, take-care-of-business darker-hued Black woman *type*. But the producer seemed to imply that it would be *unbelievable*, that it would strain the credulity as well as the colorist prejudice of the television audience to cast these sisters in roles outside the stereotype. Film and media critic George Alexander argues that the most pressing issue facing Black actors is the paucity of interesting, serious roles for them to play, no matter what their complexion. But the fact remains that while much of what we see on television is stereotypical—the bumbling husband saved from his own stupidity by the competent wife, the heroic detective or cop who bucks the system to find the killer, the dumb blonde, the vicious Black criminal—more often than not, lighter-skinned actresses *can* be cast in roles that feature them as both a love interest/the object of sexual desire and as strong, determined women.

The producer is good-natured as he takes my ribbing and we gossip about Vin Diesel's $20 million salary for the film *Triple* X. The producer says of Diesel, "Finally we got a light-skinned brother who can kick ass. Now that's casting against *type*." But I remind him that Diesel refuses even to talk about race and routinely turns aside questions about his racial identity.

The longer we talk, the more I realize what I know: that in America everything, even blackness, is designed and shaped in its public presentation to support and uphold and encourage the supremacy of whiteness. We have been talking about color and colorism, but we have also been talking about the consciousness and the imagination that activate television and much of popular culture. The producer's hesitancy was justified because the prevailing beauty ethic and the way it is upheld is brutal and consistent, and exceptions to it merely prove the rule. He didn't want to reveal industry secrets. He didn't want to break the silence because, as a Black man in the industry, there is pitifully little that he can do to change it.

On the television doctor drama *Presidio Med*, actress Anna Deavere Smith is sitting in a bar with several other women doctors after a hard day at the hospital. Over drinks they are comparing notes on what they like in a man. Deavere Smith, at the end of a fairly long list, smiles and says, "And he's got to have good hair."

I am watching my guilty pleasure, HBO's *Sex and the City*. This Sunday night I am watching the Black actress Lisa Gay Hamilton play a neighbor to Miranda, who has just had a baby and can't get the infant to stop crying. The character played by Hamilton knocks on Miranda's door to complain about the noise and spends the rest of the show teaching Miranda how to stop the baby's whining and fretting. I sit cringing at this waste of a wonderful actress in a role that smacks of a mammy, painfully aware that a lighter-skinned actress would never have been cast in anything this close to "birthin' babies."

Mirror on the Wall

Mirror, Mirror on The Wall
Who's the Finest of them All?
Snow White, you black bitch,
And Don't You Forget it.

—"MIRROR, MIRROR," FROM THE *AIN'T JOKIN'*
SERIES, 1987–88; ARTIST: CARRIE WEEMS

"When people walk into a room and see Halle," says
Warren Beatty, who cast her in Bulworth, "they always
laugh. They don't know how else to react. They're
not used to seeing someone that beautiful."

—FROM "THE BEAUTIFUL AND DAMNED: HALLE
BERRY OVERCOMES HER LOOKS IN 'MONSTER'S
BALL,'" *NEW YORK TIMES MAGAZINE*

What does it mean to be Black and beautiful? I am reading Donald Bogle's book *Brown Sugar: Eighty Years of America's Black Female Superstars*, and on the pages of this marvelous history of Black female icons of film, stage, and music I see confirmation of my mother's assertion that God had made Black women in America beautiful in more ways than any other women on earth. When she said this, always making the statement with pride and amazement, I often bitterly thought of how we became a race of women whose beauty resides in so many different skin tones and types of features. I thought of the Middle Passage, of slavery, and of the sexual exploitation and rape of enslaved women. I thought of New Orleans Creoles, octoroons, quadroons, and mulattoes.

The idea that Black is beautiful remains controversial, questioned, and doubted. Even as Black women's magazines have begun routinely featuring darker-skinned models, and as African models like Alek Wek from Sudan, Liya Kebede from Ethiopia, and Oluchi from Nigeria grace the pages and covers of *Vogue, Elle,* and other women's fashion glossies in America and abroad, the question still remains: *Is Black beautiful?*

The beauty of light women often seems more legitimate because it is closer to the standards propagated by Whites. But Black people may also feel that same beauty carries the "stigma" of Whiteness. Except in the cases of children born of consensual interracial relationships or interracial marriages, we may feel that to look on a light-skinned Black woman is to see her great-great-grandmother who was the sexual companion or the sexual victim of some anonymous or forgotten White man. Or her great-great-grandfather, who secretly bedded a White woman.

Some of us look at light skin and feel lifted, physically

lightened, perhaps exalted, just by gazing at it. We process that skin shade through all the conscious and subconscious positive meanings and attributes of lightness the society and the culture has imposed.

We feel conflicting emotions about the beauty of dark women. We look at that face and see everything that racism, the enemy not yet fully evicted from our minds and hearts, has defined as ugly. Darkness makes us think of the past too, of an Africa we may know nothing of and care nothing about. That we may mock or even despise. An Africa that is synonymous with poverty, not power or pride. We look at dark skin that is unmitigated and un-apologetically, *purely* dark, and perhaps we resist it. Some invisible screen descends to separate us from it and all the negative meanings and attributes of darkness the society and the culture has imposed.

How do we unravel the web of undesirable associations and assumptions and the sinister construction of blackness as an idea that make it impossible for us to embrace the root and the essence of what we are? Asserting that "Black is beautiful" is but a first step on a journey that will require that we gaze at ourselves with new eyes. Eyes created by a new mind. The journey will be traumatic and shattering, arduous and frightening. What would our Black female icon look like if she was chosen with an imagination freed from the shackles of self-hatred? If we measured every as-pect of this symbolic personage with a sensibility reclaimed from those who had hijacked and poisoned it? If we cele-brated every part of our African/Black/African American selves that we reflexively deny, then she would be a dark-skinned Black woman. We would have to enter the place that we don't want to go. We would have to journey back to where we began. African Americans are the great equivocators in the continuing discussion about color. *"But I'm one-quarter Cherokee." "My grandfather was Irish." "How can only black be beautiful when we come in come so many shades?" "Look at the whole continent of Africa—you'll see light skin and straight hair there too."* Embracing and loving the blackness, the darkness from which we sprang (because most African Americans are descended from darker-skinned, broad-featured West Africans) is like taking the first gulp of air to ensure life. Looking into its depth, seeing its power and its glory. Until we manage to do this, quite frankly we will never be free.

I sit studying two classic photos in the Bogle book. First there is the famous photo of Bessie Smith, the 1920s Empress of the Blues. She is posed wearing a long elegant evening gown and standing before parted curtains on a stage, a wide grin animating her brown face. There is so much radiance and power in her confident stare. I see the wide, nearly flat nose, the cheekbones that are not high but low, the lips, broad, unmistakable, and that as she smiles, are shaped like a valentine. Bessie Smith's brows are thick and determined. She is buxom and full-figured. I can almost feel the excitement that Smith must have generated and the charisma she exuded when she strutted on-stage and sang blues tunes with lyrics that were overtly and brazenly sexual. Songs like "Put It Right Here (Or Keep It

Out There)," "Need a Little Sugar in My Bowl," "I'm Wild About That Thing," and "You Gotta Give Me Some."

Then I turn to the photo of Lena Horne, singer and actress, defined in the words of Bogle as a gorgeous "mulatto type" whose career spanned more than fifty years. Bogle says, "In the history of American popular entertainment, no woman had ever looked like Lena Horne. Nor had any other black woman had looks considered as safe and nonthreatening. She had color, a rich glowing coppertone. She wasn't too dark or too light. Her hair was straight. She was labeled café au lait. . . . When she first started to perform, she was even urged to change her name and pass as Latin."

Lena Horne in the past and Halle Berry today are Black women whose racially mixed heritage makes them, in the eyes of many, more beautiful than either a woman defined as White or one defined as Black. I say *defined* because most of us in America are racial mongrels. It is estimated, for example, that 40 percent of "White" Americans have "Black" ancestors that they know nothing of or choose not to acknowledge. The mixture of ethnicities, races, tongues, and tribes that a biracial woman symbolizes, with its hints of sex and domination, submission, and the fusing of White and Black or White and brown, provides just enough color to be interesting but not enough to be offensive.

When we look at the photo of Bessie Smith, we are gazing at her through the psychic outline of Lena Horne that fills our minds. The small nose. The thin lips. The "fair" skin. *This*, we think, is real beauty. We can't help it.

But we cannot possibly create a legitimate standard of Black female beauty that springs from and owes its inspiration to White beauty. Despite the White blood that flows through our veins, we cannot have it both ways. Having it both ways means accommodating and honoring the White and the brown in us and turning our backs on the Black.

Having it both ways means arguing that because we are a "mixed-race" people, rejection of dark-hued skin is inevitable, a natural outcome. As though self-hatred were "natural."

Halle Berry now occupies the exalted position of mulatto beauty in Hollywood that Lena Horne once held. Her combination of talent, drive, and a type of beauty that is acceptable to the cultural powerbrokers and the movie-going audience at large has given her options unprecedented for an African American actress. But the near rapturous anointing of Berry as a safe and acceptable symbol of beauty and sexuality is rooted in Whites' perception of her as much more White than Black.

The European standard of beauty reigns and rules the world because it is an extension of White political and economic power. It also rules because Whites are willing without hesitation to define what they mean by beauty. But as African Americans we are unwilling to clearly define and hold on to a notion of Black beauty that is not merely an extension of White standards, one that makes room for Black women who span the spectrum. We do not want to say that full lips, black skin, and a broad nose, typically West African features, are our standard. We do not possess an autonomous sense of beauty, one unconnected to our history of oppression.

"Their union violates societal norms about black beauty and white male potency," said Dr. Robert T. Carter, a professor of psychology at Teachers College, Columbia University, who has written extensively on racial identity.
—FROM A *NEW YORK TIMES* ARTICLE ABOUT THE ROMANCE BETWEEN ACTORS WHOOPI GOLDBERG AND TED DANSON

Andrea: I see a lot of girls in the media with beautiful faces and long, straight hair. They have this mad Coke-bottle shape and I'm like Oh, I want to look like that. I want to look like Angelina Jolie. Her face is so exotic. And when I see other girls, especially the so-called video hos, they're so cute. They aren't model thin, they're kind of thick, but they're still cute. I would be sexy and attractive and cute. And everyone would want me.
—FROM "LUNCH WITH LATIFAH," A ROUND TABLE WITH SEVEN TEEN GIRLS CONDUCTED BY QUEEN LATIFAH IN *ESSENCE* MAGAZINE

Heartthrob never. Black and ugly as ever.
—FROM "ONE MORE CHANCE" BY NOTORIOUS B.I.G.

When I stood before the mirror as a child, an adolescent, and a young woman, while the mirror was not neutral, it captured my preferred self-image. That image might have been me at ten with my mother's scarves draped over my head, fantasizing that I had long straight hair, or me at nineteen wearing an Afro. The mirror was not neutral, because I brought to the mirror all the various constructions of beauty that raged in my mind. I looked in the mirror and saw not what was there but what I believed was there.

Today young Black girls, influenced by a relentless and steady diet of music videos, find themselves gazing into a cruel, pitiless mirror that like all mass media packages sexuality and beauty in the most homogenized way and that invalidates any expressions of beauty that deviate from the established "norm."

The plaintive, heartrending desire of Andrea, the young woman quoted from the *Essence* round table, to look like a video "ho" cannot be blamed entirely on the influence of music videos. Clearly the messages about beauty and the undesirability of dark skin bloom hardiest in the minds of girls who may have never been told by a parent or a family member that they are attractive and worthy *just as they are*. Only parents and family members who possess a healthy image of themselves can speak those words to their children. Too often even parents who feel worthy, mothers who feel beautiful, fail to raise their children on the kind of dialogues that will create self-worth.

The videos establish a standard, but it is one that merely reflects everything else that Andrea sees and hears. The videos operate within a complex and interconnected system. As an African American teen, Andrea most likely watches videos aired on Black Entertainment Television, a station founded by an African American entrepreneur. The videos dramatize what she may already suspect, that as a Black girl she is considered neither alluring nor pretty unless she is light and long-haired. The videos feature wealthy, talented Black singers of all skin tones as the carriers of this subliminal but often overt message. It's not just that Andrea needs to turn off the music videos. She needs people—parents and even peers—who will give her permission to challenge the dominance of one vision of beauty and assert her unique inner worth and outer sense of style.

Cultural historian Anthony Browder says of Black youths' fascination with and near addiction to music videos, "BET has set us back a decade. There simply are not enough messages in the rest of the culture to counter the self-hating propaganda that most of the videos present."

Browder writes about African history and travels throughout the United States and abroad presenting lectures, symposiums, and video presentations on African and African American history and culture.

For Browder, music videos are as lethal as racism, poverty, and crime in their impact on the Black community and the self-esteem of African American youths. And what he calls the "gradual Europeanization" of the physical appearance of pop king Michael Jackson has resulted in dire and damaging consequences on the vulnerable and emerging identities of adolescent Blacks.

"You have to remember that Michael Jackson essentially invented the music video as we know it," Browder says. "It was his 1984 video 'Thriller' that put him on top and established the music video as a new and highly profitable vehicle for promoting music. I think that after the unprecedented success of 'Thriller' he decided to change his appearance to appeal to the widest possible audience— the whole planet. What followed was three nose jobs, four chin jobs, the widening of his eyes, and the alteration of his skin so that now he resembles nothing as much as a grotesque parody of Whiteness."

"But it's more than a parody of Whiteness," I tell Browder. "Michael Jackson is a parody of Black folks' love affair with Whiteness, the desire, sometimes secret and unexpressed, other times obvious and acknowledged, that lots of us still have to be lighter and whiter than we are. We are ashamed of him not just because he brought all the color neurosis straight out of the closet, but because he wanted to be White and he had enough money to actually turn into his vision of Whiteness."

"No doubt we remain brain damaged on the issue of color," he says. "I think it is symbolically very significant that Michael Jackson, after introducing a vehicle, the music video, that promotes colorism and the supremacy of White standards of beauty, proceeds then to remove any and all vestiges of his identity as a Black man."

In his presentations before audiences of Black students in schools and colleges, Browder says that he presents a variety of images of African peoples, from ancient time to the present. "It creates a sense of pride in these young people when they see images of African rulers who were, in their time, among the most powerful people on earth. They see themselves as players in history, and they see themselves more positively."

But in order to challenge the dominant notions of beauty and to talk about Black identity, Browder says he also presents before and after images of popular Black entertainers who have had their features "Whitened." Students are always surprised at how many Black entertainers have had their features modified, and Browder says that he talks about the meaning of this and what it says about Black identity. How altering "Black" features seems to be a requirement for some people to have crossover success.

You don't look like an American idol.
—AMERICAN *IDOL* JUDGE SIMON COWELL
TO A FULL-FEATURED, HEAVYSET
BROWN-SKINNED FEMALE SINGER VYING
TO BE CHOSEN AS A FINALIST

During a 1999 story for "48 Hours" on a teenager
in jail, Goldberg says, a New York producer
asked his field producer, "What is she?"
"She's black," the producer told his boss in New York,
"but she's light-skinned." He felt he had to say that
to get the okay to proceed with the story.
—FROM "EX-CORRESPONDENT LETS LOOSE IN
BOOK ON CBS," *WASHINGTON POST*

For the dark-skinned black woman it comes as a series of
disappointments and embarrassments that the wives of
virtually all black leaders (including Marcus Garvey) appear
to have been chosen for the nearness of their complexions to
white alone. . . . Because it is apparent that though they
may have consciously affirmed blackness in the abstract and
for others, for themselves light remained right.

—ALICE WALKER

For Browder, the 2001 release of the album *Acoustic Soul* by singer India.Arie marks a watershed moment in entertainment and social history. "The album is so important because it's clearly a response to the crazy world that the music videos present and their harmful effects. The album gives me hope. Whenever the pendulum swings so far in one direction, there's got to be a reaction."

The day that I first heard India.Arie's song "Video" began with a conversation about color. That morning I visited my adult stepdaughter and as we talked, sitting on her bed, BET offered up a sample of video hits by Black hip-hop and rap stars. I commented on the absence of brown or dark-skinned girls in the videos, and Keesha shared with me her disillusionment with much of what she saw on the video jukeboxes for that reason. Then she told me that there was a new song and video out by a singer named India.Arie. It was a video, she assured me, that I would like. "The next time it's played, I'll give you a call so you can see it," she promised.

Later that evening Keesha called me and said simply, "Turn to *Rap City*. They're playing the video I told you about."

In a sea of videos that featured images of Black violence, grotesqueness, confusion, Black female singers bragging about their sexual exploits, comparing themselves to whores, darker-skinned Black women as the object of degradation, row after row of long-haired, light-skinned model types, Asian and Latina and White girls draped over the gold-swathed Black rapper—into this madness stepped India.Arie singing an entirely different tune. Arie, tall, lanky, dark, broad-nosed and dreadlocked, presented an alternate image of beauty, a black one that was African inspired.

Arie deconstructs traditional video mythology with an anthem of her own called "Video," which asserts, "I'm not the average girl from your video / And I ain't built like a supermodel / But I learned to love myself unconditionally / Because I am a queen / I'm not the average girl from your video / My worth is not determined by the price of my clothes . . . / When I look in the mirror the only one there is me / Every freckle on my face is where it's supposed to be / And I know our creator didn't make no mistakes on me / My feet, my thighs, my lips, my eyes, I'm lovin' what I see."

Never once in this song does India.Arie mention color. She doesn't have to. It's the subtext of the song. I sat on my living room sofa enthralled, vindicated, stunned, affirmed by the sight of this beautiful and, I knew even then, brave young woman. The young woman stealing my heart through the TV screen was dark, she was tall (*too tall for a girl*), full-featured, and with the flowers in her hair and her happy-go-lucky charm I couldn't tell if she was a hippie or a seer. But I knew what it had cost her to write that song. I knew instinctively, even before I read the scores of magazine articles that would soon follow in the wake of her success, what it had meant to be India.Arie: It meant having a beauty that few people saw, not fitting in any box that existed, and deciding to make a box of your own, one that fit your specifications and that allowed you to breathe.

In the weeks after I saw the video, I talked with friends whose daughters begged them to play the song repeatedly on the car stereo, or who sang it while dressing for school. Soon it was clear that India.Arie had not written a song. She had penned an anthem. And then there is "Brown Skin," the second hit from her debut CD, a funky, throbbing ode to the beauty of brown skin that establishes Arie as not just a wonderful new voice but as truth teller and truth seeker, a young woman who wants to use music and lyrics for more than booty shakin' or singing the same old love song.

But the 2002 Grammy Awards pit Arie against Alicia Keys, whose song "Fallin'" established her as another major new voice. Both sisters were talented. Both had paid some serious dues to get where they are. But like it or not, the competition took on the appearance of a battle between the "biracial beauty" (Keys) backed by record mogul Clive Davis, who debuted "Fallin'" on *Oprah* and *Good*

Morning America, versus the "soul sister" (Arie), who wore head wraps and whose album was as political and threatening to conventional White-supremacist wisdom as anything I had heard in years. Keys and Arie represented virtual poles on the spectrum of African American female beauty. Keys, sultry and ethnically ambiguous, in her photos often projected a come-hither or tough-girl stance; Arie, deep, dark brown, possessed an air of ethereal wisdom and innocence.

I rooted for India.Arie because of the courage it took to write "Video" and her ode to the African American body, "Brown Skin." *Acoustic Soul* was medicine for the battered, wounded spirits of so many of my sisters and brothers. But I was too cynical even to think that India.Arie would win even one of the seven Grammys she was nominated for. During the weeks leading up to the Grammy Awards I couldn't stop thinking: *Whites buy most of the world's CDs; they own the record companies and choreograph and cast the videos. I know that even in the videos of "Black" singers I am not the primary intended audience. We're talking a global billion-dollar industry. We're talking not music but sex and fantasies and dreams and who can sell more of all that. We are talking not just who has a great voice but who can represent what the world believes is beautiful and valuable and worth having.*

I convinced myself that India.Arie wouldn't win. Couldn't win, all so I wouldn't be disappointed. Still, I crossed the fingers of my heart. *Maybe they'll give her one?* I felt as if I were being judged, like all brown to black women everywhere would somehow win or lose on Grammy Awards night.

At the Grammy Awards India.Arie heard her name read seven times, and each time someone else won, and five times it was Alicia Keys. I hated that it had come to this. Two beautiful and talented Black women who just wanted to sing their songs symbolizing the color complex. In the days that followed the Grammys there was anger and disappointment among Arie's fans. The Internet and the radio station call-in shows buzzed with the question "Was Arie ripped off 'cause she's dark and Keys is light?" But amid the controversy, I was heartened because at least I heard folks talking about "the light/dark thang," acknowledging it in ways that were new and unfamiliar. We were having a public conversation we had been afraid to have for a very long time. India.Arie had helped us to form the first words.

In the aftermath of her very public disappointment, Arie took the high road and talked openly of the spiritual lessons learned from the loss. And she became a kind of folk hero, valorous and loved even more by her fans for her grace and spirit. She lost the competition but passed the only test that, in the end, really mattered to me.

Sisters Under the Skin

*It doesn't matter if we're light or if we are dark,
we all feel like we're not enough of who we are
because we are always being pursued, attacked, or
rejected because of what we look like.*

—THERAPIST AUDREY CHAPMAN

And yet we are sisters. Sisters under the skin. Sisters because of the skin. I have spoken of distances and differences. Of separate realities, of preferences and denial of self. Of visible and invisible barricades that seem to place Black women of different colors on opposite sides in the same battle. The battle to exist and find expression as women recognized as complex and contradictory, as valuable and necessary. The battle to love ourselves so much that what the world gives or denies us doesn't matter.

I have had intense, enormously satisfying friendships

with several very light-skinned Black women. Those relationships came to resemble sisterhood. Some of the most revealing conversations I ever had about the color complex I had with these women. These were women who could joke about the pitfalls and the pleasures of being "high yellow" and call themselves that name with affectionate derision. Women who taught me that we were indeed different sides of the same shimmering, mysterious moon. Women who had been bequeathed by parents or who managed to sculpt on their own a private language and a sensibility that honored Black identity in its multitude of expressions.

One of these women once said to me that she felt that among Black women the strongest bonds were actually between women who were either very dark-skinned or very light. Her argument was that the extreme, often excessive reactions that those hues inspired made these women's experiences very similar.

While dark women can be rendered invisible, the objectification and hypersexualization of light women imposes a kind of invisibility on them as well. And in both cases the women suffer considerable pain.

TaRessa Stovall is a biracial forty-something writer and PR consultant who lives in New Jersey. Her mother is Jewish and her father is Black. "I have been mistaken for virtually anything you can name, Greek, Mexican, Arab, Puerto Rican," she told me. "I went to mostly white schools as a young child, but when I entered junior high school, the school was racially mixed. I remember being in the bathroom one day and all the little Black girls fawning over me and admiring my hair, how long and straight it was. I felt a mixture of emotions. I was pleased, I guess, to be the center of attention, but even then I knew that it was too intense. I knew that there was something not quite right about the way the girls responded to me. The funny thing is that the next year the Afro was in style and I couldn't get one because my hair was too straight. Then the same girls who had been fawning over me rejected me because I literally looked like Marlo Thomas. Nothing I did would change my hair.

"When I got to high school, my running buddies, my two closest girlfriends, were much darker than I, and both were very pretty. I was so gawky and chubby that they got way more attention from boys than I did. I wasn't popular or desired at the time. But I slimmed down, spruced up, and learned how to flirt. That made a big difference.

"You are considered a prize—there's no way of getting around it—when you have *the look*. You get a lot of attention. You are treated special and like you are pretty. I've always felt flattered but I also felt a lot of angst. I mean, it's just skin and hair, and so after a while as I got older I began to realize that men were reacting not to who I was but how I looked. This is all pretty heavy stuff for a young girl or a teenager to navigate her way through. It's easy to become insecure, to not know a man's real motives."

At this point I share with TaRessa my feeling that the color complex makes a victim of lighter-skinned women by objectifying them and oversexualizing them at a very young age.

"I remember when I was in high school," I tell her. "There were two sisters who I knew. Lillian was the oldest, a year older than her sister Denise. Lillian had light brown skin, keen features, and a head full of jet black straight hair. Her sister Denise was very pretty too, but she was darker. She was slender, had beautiful eyes, and her dark skin was absolutely flawless. But Denise carried herself like someone who had been beaten down, who had not an ounce of confidence. She slouched, she wore a perpetual scowl, and at sixteen was neurotic and a nervous wreck. It was pretty obvious to everyone what the problem was. Lillian got all the attention from the boys in school, and I mean all the attention. They wore her out with the jockeying for her favor, the catcalls in the hallway, begging for her phone number. And they looked right through Denise when the two were together like she wasn't even there. I could understand Denise's anguish, but what puzzled me then was Lillian's misery. Despite all the attention, she seemed in some ways as unhappy as her sister. I know that she was really pressured by the boys she dated to have sex, because Denise and I sometimes talked and she told me this. And as I am telling you this and looking back on those girls, I remember that Denise alternated between rage and abject passivity, as though she had already given up on life. And I remember when I was around Lillian sensing that she felt somehow that her life was already out of her hands, that it belonged to the boys who pursued her, that it didn't belong to her."

"I've never heard the dynamic put that way, objectification and hypersexualized," TaRessa says, "but I think that's a good way to describe what happens. I remember going out to parties or clubs with my best friend, who was dark-skinned, when I was single, and it was always so hard because the men would be falling all over me and ignoring her. And the irony was and is that she is truly drop-dead gorgeous and I'm pretty average at best. And so often I knew with me it was the hair and skin, and that didn't make me feel good. It caused some tension in our friendship, but the relationship survived. It got to a point where I began to test my boyfriends to see if they were color-struck. I'd try to find out who they dated before me, to see if they only dated light-skinned women. I became very blunt, very outspoken, in response to the way people reacted to the way I look. I developed that as a defense mechanism. Either people try to challenge my Blackness or they assume certain things about me because of how I look. I just got tired of it and will read folks the riot act in a minute."

TaRessa has a son and a daughter, and when I asked her how she talks to them about color, with characteristic bluntness TaRessa said that she has told her daughter, "You have the kind of looks that people get way too excited about. I want you to know that often it's not really about you. It's just about how you look, and that isn't real."

For photographer Tricia Warley, the journey through the color complex has been fraught with pain and has required acts of courage that have alienated her from much of her family. Raised in Nashville, Tennessee, Tricia described a childhood of unbearable contradictions:

> *Quite frankly, my parents urged me to be colorist.*
> *Because I am so light and my hair is so straight, I was*
> *often told that I had "high genes" and "blow hair," and*
> *that is what distinguished me from the "jigaboos," the*
> *derogatory name for dark-skinned Blacks my parents*
> *often used. The irony was that on the surface, my father*
> *was really what you would call a "race man" in terms of*
> *his activism to bring about equality for Blacks and social*
> *change. But whenever he caught me playing with the*
> *darker-skinned children in our neighborhood, he'd beat*
> *me and tell me "I don't ever want to see you going home*
> *with those niggers again." I have relatives who range*
> *from very light to very dark. My father is light, my*
> *mother is olive-toned, I am very light and my brother*
> *looks White. My parents claimed race pride to the*
> *outside world but behind closed doors they were intensely*
> *colorist. Out of one side of their mouth they talked civil*
> *rights and out of the other, they talked color prejudice.*
> *This was the horrible schizophrenia that ruled our home.*
> *But somehow from childhood, I always embraced*
> *Blackness, and was proud of my African genes.*
>
> *As a child I loved to dance, loved Black music,*
> *loved to laugh, all the things associated in my family with*
> *dark-skinned Blacks. And no amount of punishment,*
> *and there was plenty of it, could change me. I was a*

major disappointment to my parents, who hated my identification with Blackness, and love of Black culture. And yet, it was always so hard, and to some extent even today, remains hard for me to be accepted by other Blacks. I still encounter darker-skinned sisters who assume I feel superior to them because of my color.

I attended Howard in the sixties, where I was a social activist, and a militant. Of course I noticed that the light girls got all the attention. And I got my share of attention too, which was hard for me despite my commitment to the movement. I was a loner, I think to some extent as a response to the suspicion that often greeted me because of my light skin, but that never dampened my progressive politics or my willingness to identify as Black and work on behalf of Black people.

In my relationships with men so often my hair and color got in the way, and lots of brothers simply couldn't go deeper than that. But with my husband that wasn't an issue. He got beyond the exterior, but we faced challenges in other areas. I have been a Buddhist for twenty years and a lot has changed in my life and in my consciousness as a result. Several years ago I got dreadlocks, and it was a decision I made to make my life easier. I got tired of playing games with men, of them telling me I looked like someone in a magazine, of them not being able to see "me" for my light skin and straight hair. When I locked my hair I found that a lot of that craziness stopped. The locks force brothers to look at me, to try to see who I really am. The locks make me less of

*a sex object. Fewer men come on to me now, but I feel I
have gained a more liberated sense of myself and an
easier way of living in the world. I wear dreads, wear
African clothing, consider myself Afrocentric and the
price I have paid is rejection by my family. But I couldn't
live any other way.*

Audrey Chapman is the author of several books on Black
male-female relationships, a therapist at the Howard University counseling center, and the host of a popular radio
talk show that focuses on male-female relationship issues.
I wanted to talk to Chapman about colorism because as a
mental health professional she spends much of her time
talking to Black women about their lives, their desires,
their dreams, and their deepest wounds. She is a woman
who counseled me out of a pattern of unfulfilling relationships with men and helped me to realize a healthy sense of
self that made it possible for me to create a space in my life
for my husband, Joe.

Over a brown-bag lunch of salads in her office,
Chapman and I catch up on my life and hers. Her small office is cluttered with books and papers, a sign of the hectic,
busy nature of her life. "How did you decide to write this
book?" she asks as she settles into a comfortable chair and
places her salad on her lap.

"In a way I've been writing it all my life," I tell her.
"I've wanted to deal with the subject for a very long time,
but until now I didn't know how."

"I didn't know how," I tell Audrey, and think as I say

this that each day, with each conversation, I am trying to learn how to tell this story. I am learning as I read a book about the great Black writer Paul Laurence Dunbar and discover how deeply scarred he was by colorism, how much he hated his dark black skin and Negroid features. I am learning as I read the short stories of Charles Chesnutt and about the history of Blacks in Cuba. I am trying to find a way to speak what has been for most of my life, for me, unspeakable. I don't tell Audrey how I sit before the computer screen and feel the pages of this book wrung out of my flesh, ripped from the bowels of my most secret, secret place.

I have wanted to write this book for a very long time. And now that I am writing it, there is nowhere for me to run. Nowhere for me to hide. Audrey is a therapist, and this day as we talk, will I tell her how angry it makes me to see so few brown to black women exalted in the media? Will I ask her if maybe I am defensive, too sensitive? Why I can't let the color thing be? I can't let it be because I know it's about more than Gregory not wanting to touch me in fifth grade, and pretty brown boys looking past me to the light-skinned girls. I can't let it go because it's about money, as I discover when I read an essay that says that a study found that dark-skinned African Americans are paid on average 25 percent less than light-skinned Blacks. I can't let it go because it's about access, as one of my former students reminds me when recalling his days at Princeton he tells me that most of the Black students there were either biracial or light-skinned. It's about a diversity trainer for several major corporations telling me that she feels ambivalent because she benefits from light-skinned privilege and says that it's sad but true that Whites simply feel more comfortable around lighter-skinned Blacks. And I guess that means I have spent my life making Whites feel uncomfortable, maybe scaring the shit out of them with my brown skin and short Afro and attitude. I can't let it go because it's about opportunity, as I remember reading an article in *Essence* about African American actresses and the dearth of opportunities in Hollywood and how one dark-skinned actress was told by a White producer that she wouldn't find much work because she was "nigger black." No, I can't let it go, and I won't let it be.

I sat in this same room twelve years ago, and I never told you about my mother's admonition. For if I told you I would have to reveal the anger I have borne so long. Anger at my mother. I told you everything about everything except my color complex. Why should I? Surely it hadn't held me back. It hadn't kept me down. It didn't derail my dreams. But I wonder how much higher I might have soared without it. And if I told you about my mother's words I would have to let go of the good girl she raised me to be, the girl with table manners and "home training" who was a good-student, make-all-the-family-proud girl, who would never, ever let her mother know how deeply those words cut. How deeply they hurt. The good girl who rationalized and understood and explained away the words over the years, words that seeped into me like a lethal injection.

I came to you to learn how to bring real love into my life, love that would last, love for myself and love for someone else. I joked that you planned to work roots on me, as you promised that by the time we finished, I would find love, because I would know love and I would in fact be love. And six months after I left your office for the last time as a client, I met Joe, the one I was waiting for. The one I was waiting to be big enough for. The one who taught me love always arrives on time.

But I never told you about my dark-skinned-Black-woman anger. I never told you about my love/hate affair with Sapphire and Beulah. I was politically conscious, still wore an Afro, and that was then this was now. Surely those women had no hold on me. Surely those women had nothing to do with my fear that I wasn't good enough for a good man. Surely not. Surely not.

And talking to you on this day, I don't tell you how I wonder at my brown-skinned-woman anger, wonder at its ferocity, its loyalty, its stubbornness. I don't tell you how I dread it and yet how it fuels me. How justified I feel it is and how I will never let it go. How it occupies me like a quiet eternal flame and like an arrogant army of conquest. I love my light-skinned sisters and deeply resent their privilege. I love this anger that has driven me to write this book as a prayer and a scream and a poem to my sisters dark and light. I hate this anger for the ways it sets me apart and chokes me on questions that seem to have no answer I can live with or repeat. I love this anger, for it fuels every friendship I have with a light-skinned sister when I feel we are residents of the same skin—a woman's skin and that's all that matters. I hate this anger, for it is my legacy and my obstacle course. I love this anger, for every book I have ever written has sprung from a question or a wound.

Well, what can I tell you?" Chapman asks.

"What do you see in your practice? How do your clients reflect the impact of the color complex?"

"I have so many women who come in to see me, and when we start examining where their low self-esteem springs from it's all about hair or skin color or features. They'll tell me, 'I had the nappiest hair. I was the darkest one in the family,' and they feel that they were treated differently because of that. Women come to me and want to discuss their desire to have their lips made thinner and their noses made smaller. They are so unsure of themselves. What I try to tell these women is that they will still be the same woman inside after the surgery.

"It's not only darker women who come to me with issues related to colorism. Light-skinned women can become very insecure because they have depended on men to tell them they are beautiful. And yet behind this dependency is a great deal of insecurity because so much emphasis has been placed on their looks rather than what they are inside. Light-skinned women can be so used to being pursued for how they look that they are often confused about who they really are. And they have relationship problems as severe as dark women's. Light women can be victims of tremendous sexual exploitation. Men will just run through them because they see them as a conquest."

"It's really interesting how pervasive that is," I say. "I conducted some interviews with a group of high school seniors and several college freshman, male and female.

And I was really amazed by the ways that lighter-skinned women are demonized and sexualized. The young men would readily admit that they rarely used the word *pretty* to describe even the most attractive dark girl. One young man said, 'We'll say that a light girl is pretty and a dark-skinned girl is okay.' Yet despite that, both males and females often called light girls 'freaks,' implied or just flat-out stated that light-skinned girls were promiscuous. It seems that light women are pursued as sex objects, and once they respond to that designation they are labeled in a way that damages them, despite the assumed advantage of light skin and 'good' hair."

"Well, look at the videos," Chapman says. "That's pretty much how the light-skinned girls are portrayed, as sexual freaks, desired but dominated by the male in the story line."

But what concerns Chapman as well is what she calls the "sea change" in the Black community around definitions of beauty and aging. She reaches to a nearby table for a local magazine distributed on Howard's campus that focuses on women's health issues, turns to the back, and points to a page of listings and advertisements placed by Black plastic surgeons. Shaking her head in dismay she says, "Black women are now heavily into plastic surgery—tummy tucks, breast implants, liposuction, and nose jobs. We've launched a frenzy of lightening and whitening that I don't understand. And the blond hair. I woke up one morning and suddenly half the Black women I know are blondes."

"Times have changed," I say. "Lots of Black women feel blonde is a color they can claim. We've got more disposable income and like everybody else in the culture we want to be young and thin."

"Well, times have changed and they haven't. To go back to your conversation with those high school seniors and college kids, I think that a lot of Black parents are dropping the ball on this issue—they simply are not talking about it with their children."

"But young people talk about color quite a lot it seems," I tell her. "These same young people that demonized and glorified light girls also dissected the colorism of the videos. The young women found the blatantly colorist casting offensive. The young people I've talked to are all over the spectrum in their attitudes. Some think Lil' Kim's blond wig is 'just hair,' nothing more. Others I spoke with saw it as a denial of her identity. If there is anything that was revealed by the conversations I had with young people it's that they know they are both victims and perpetrators of colorism. They know they're being dissed, they just don't know what to do about it."

Howard has long had a reputation for colorism, so I asked Chapman what she sees on the campus now. "From conversations with female students I gather that there has been some change, but light-skinned girls still rule from what female students tell me. And there seems to be a narrowing of what it means to be attractive. You see a few dreads, and naturals and braids, but an awful lot of bone straight hair."

"But, Audrey, what are these young women to do?" I ask. "I talked with a friend last week who had just signed a petition protesting the firing of a Black woman from her position of some authority at a major corporation because she refused to get rid of her braids. They were deemed too ethnic. When Black women assert their racial heritage through hairstyles and dress, the corporate world that they want to be a part of gives them the boot. And if they straighten their hair some folks say they aren't 'Black' enough. How do we ever win?"

I conduct a round-table discussion for *Essence* on the often difficult relations between White and Black women in the corporate world, and about the challenges of rising to the top. Not until days after the round table do I realize that of the women who participated in the discussion, those who had managed to remain in the business world were light. The women who left in frustration to start their own businesses were dark.

Postcards from the Edge of the Color Complex

All my brothers and I married dark-skinned women. We felt like, coming from our family, which was so pale, we needed the color. I guess you could say we took

*the color complex in the other direction. I just found
brown-skinned women really pretty.*

—LONNIE

*My parents literally warned me to stay away from "those
black boys" when I was in high school. And their
message was loud and clear. Black equaled danger.
Those boys were no good. If I got involved with a black
boy I would come to no good. And they were to be
avoided because they were dark.*

—ALISON

*My parents raised my brother and me on the "I'm Black
and proud" ethic. And they drummed it into us, with
conversations, educational and cultural experiences,
travel, books, everything. Coming from a dark-skinned
family, one that was economically privileged, Black pride
was a good armor to have, especially knowing that
not everyone felt that way.*

—DOUG

*Of course when a girl is dark and lacks much fashion sense
because most of her time is spent on the tennis court,
ridicule is never far away. I was constantly harassed
because of my black black skin by a boy who was even
darker than I was. Other times, aside from "Oreo"
(due to the way I spoke), I was called just plain ugly.
And I wasn't too young to notice that the women revered*

on television, in movies, in videos, magazines, and every
other media tended to lean to the light-skinned side. All
the same, I was never embarrassed by my skin color. I
always loved it. For what purpose would it serve to hate
something about myself that will never change?
Once in a while I want to say, "I wish I were dark, so dark
that you couldn't see me at night. Dark skin is lovely."
I'd think, "I have no dream of being fair."

—NNEDI

From "America in Black and White: Shades of Prejudice,"
a *Nightline* special report:

Michel McQueen: For example, the African-American
correspondents at ABC News are overwhelmingly light-
skinned, and their personal experiences reflect the
enduring power of the subject today.

First correspondent: When I was dating the woman
who would eventually become my wife, I was deemed
acceptable by her family mainly because of the color of
my skin or the hue of my skin. [It] was assumed [that]
A) [I was] someone who would be successful, B) [I was]
someone who was smart, and C) the babies would come
out just right.

Second correspondent: I was late getting on camera
because I honestly, you know, as much as I like myself
and think of myself as being very much TV, you know, I
felt that somehow I wouldn't be accepted because I was
too dark.

---

*The kids whose acceptance I so wanted rejected me
outright. Now, I suppose they singled me out primarily for
reasons of speech and mannerisms, but I know that being
lighter-complexioned didn't help either. That put me at
question to start with, then the rest of my personality just
sealed my fate. Ironically, some of the kids that
tormented me most were lighter than me but they made
up for it by being "Blacker" in demeanor.*

—SEAN

What do you want with me? *I'd always wonder when
I was involved with a light-skinned woman.*

—CLAUDE

I feel like I am making a psychological quilt from these
conversations. The colors are muted and vivid, the quilt
is made of lace and cotton, velvet and denim, the design is
intentional and accidental, the stuffing is all our emotional
baggage, and as in the quilts our grandmothers made, in
this quilt there are coded messages hidden inside every
stitch.

I am wrenched by heartache and exhilarated by the
communion I feel with my informants and humbled by
their confessions. After each conversation I feel bonded to
my informant in ways that are deep and abiding. Even
when people agree to talk with me only if I change their
name, still, I am all up in their business, submerged in their

psyches. They generously enter territory that has been marked off-limits for as long as they and I can remember. The more people I talk to, the more research I do, the more I am filled with compassion for myself and everyone I speak with. I am filled with awe at how all of us have been damaged and hurt, and how hard we fight, nonetheless, to go on.

From the *Nightline* special:

> *Michel McQueen: We're going to explore the theory of whether Americans in professions other than fashion and in places beyond the color-conscious South continue to judge people based on skin tone, consciously or unconsciously.*
>
> . . .
>
> *A decade ago, DePaul University Professor Midge Wilson constructed an experiment to answer this question. She was shocked by what she found out.*
>
> *Midge Wilson: We found there was a positive halo effect around the light-skinned women on various adjectives—like to what extent do you see this woman as popular, socially skilled, likely to be happy in her love life, successful, intelligent. . . . The light-skinned woman . . . received high evaluations in all these areas compared to the dark-skinned woman.*

Wilson found in her experiment that both Black and White students reacted negatively to photos of darker-skinned women. Although Wilson's willingness to conduct this experiment and discuss its findings and consequences with her students must surely be applauded, I found her alleged surprise at her findings disingenuous and wondered if it was possible for her to conduct a thoroughgoing discussion of the color complex with her students. The color complex is an outgrowth of the slave system, a three-hundred-year-long human rights violation committed against people of African descent in America.

The value and virtue of racism for White Americans is that it allows them and it even encourages them to forget their historical creation of the poisonous belief system with all its related assumptions. And if there is a slave hidden in the corners of the minds of many African Americans, there is surely a slaveholder locked behind the door in the minds of many Whites. Whites constructed the color complex and imposed a system of rewards and punishments to uphold it, and its insidious results shape nearly every aspect of life in this country, working hand in glove with racism. We live in a culture founded upon divisions of race and color, and White children imbibe a sense of racial and color superiority with every breath they take.

Wilson should not have been surprised that when her students looked at pictures of similarly dressed dark and light Black women that they defined the darker-skinned woman as less appealing and attractive. As one student concluded, "For some reason it just, with her skin tone and the darkness of it, it just looked more, I guess, slutty than it did with the lighter-skinned woman."

The color complex is a self-fulfilling, circular, and brutally deterministic ideology. Dark skin is not just considered unattractive, but it is associated with poverty, crime, anger, violence, chaos. And because the color complex was designed to discriminate against darker-skinned Blacks, to marginalize them even more completely and pervasively than lighter-skinned Blacks, because it has worked so well, its seeds have been, quite naturally, poverty, crime, anger, violence, and chaos in the lives of many more darker-skinned Blacks than in the lives of their lighter-hued brothers and sisters.

But the color complex makes everyone pay, and lighter-skinned Blacks, because of light-skinned privilege (which exists side by side with racism), become victims of suspicion and mistrust by brown to black African Americans. Emotional health, self-esteem, racial unity, and pride are all casualties of this "permanent war" that we keep waging, taking hits from outside and from within the Black community.

Grand Slam

*The Williams sisters are the higher bar in women's
tennis: fashion, style, power, precision.*
—"FOR SISTERS AMBIVALENCE OVERSHADOWS
PERFORMANCE," *NEW YORK TIMES*

They are two dark bolts of thunder, two bold flashes of brilliant, stunning darkness in a firmament that remains largely white. They are symbols of excellence, grace, athletic talent, power, and skill. They are two young Black women who have made me rethink the game of tennis, because of the ways in which they have altered the conventional wisdom about women and the game, about how to enter that world, and about what the rules of the game are. But, most important, they have made me think about my notions of brown to black women and beauty.

Her full name is Venus Ebone Starr Williams. Names assign destiny, engaging the past and the future in conversation. Names are predictions and affirmations. We live up to our names, or change them because they don't fit.

Names are poetry, philosophy. We are given names that confine us like chains and names that give us wings. In naming us, our parents invest us with their unfulfilled dreams as a way of ensuring we will be fit to shape our own.

I began using my middle name, Marita, as my first name when I left my first husband and decided that Marita was a more potent, magical, perfect name than Bernette. I'd never felt that Bernette *was* my name, for I was named to honor my mother's brother, Bernard. I wanted a name of my own. The name Marita fairly glowed in the dark. It sounded unique, memorable. It was a name that danced the samba, and it was a perfect name for a writer/woman shedding the dead skin of a life that had begun to suffocate rather than shelter. **Marita.** *I just met a girl named Marita.* Names are serious business.

When I look up the word *Venus* in the dictionary I find the following meanings: an exceptionally beautiful woman; an ancient Italian goddess of love and beauty; a goddess personifying sexual attractiveness. *Ebony* is described as "a hard, heavy durable wood, *most highly prized when black* [emphasis mine] . . . ; a deep, lustrous black"; *Starr* is "a male or female given name"; *star* is "a person's destiny, fortune, temperament . . . regarded as influenced and determined by the stars."

I am sure that Richard and Oracene Williams meant to make a star of their daughter right from the start. The names that Venus was given are weighty and momentous. Names that resonate and pulse with all our collective given knowledge of and feelings about entities and objects that we regard as valuable and desirable. These are names that are meant to elevate and challenge everyone who speaks them. Venus. Ebone. Starr. As a people who for hundreds of years were named by our oppressors, the African American community has made the act of naming an assertion of independence, a statement of culture as well as the first pronouncement of love we make to our children. Gazing at Venus when she was born, clearly the Williamses saw beauty in her baby-soft dark skin and her West African–inspired features that reflected the faces of both parents.

We know the public/family legend: Richard Williams, a fan of televised tennis, is quoted as telling his wife, Oracene, "Let's have kids and make them tennis players." Of five daughters, only the youngest two, Venus and Serena, showed promise, and they evidenced talent from the start. They were trained on public tennis courts in and around the Los Angeles suburb of Compton, an economically depressed largely Black community. Richard Williams coached his daughters on courts where they sometimes had to duck gunfire. And Williams's coaching style and the path he charted for his daughters were unconventional, but they paid off.

We know what they have achieved: As I write this Serena is ranked the number one and Venus the number two female tennis player in the world. They are the first sisters in professional tennis history to win singles titles in the same week. They became the first sisters to win a Grand Slam crown together in the twentieth century. And we know that they have made women's tennis something it had never been before: a game ruled by Black women.

Venus was the first one we knew, gangly thin, the layers of beads threaded in her hair mimicking a kind of crown. And then came Serena, the younger sister, the one with more to prove. And it is Serena who is publicly and gleefully shaping an image and a vision of herself, her femininity, and her black female beauty that is nearly revolutionary. In living rooms, huddled before the TV screens watching the Williams sisters "at work" as artistic re-creators of a game synonymous with White people, White power, and White privilege; in the barbershop soapbox pontificating about the latest White girl they have brought to her knees; stuck in traffic and looking up to see their faces on a billboard, satisfied, smiling as they advertise Avon products or Wrigley's gum; we feel pride, and maybe even a touch of their power rubs off on us. And because they are women we also inevitably, naturally, assess their beauty.

Beauty is subjective: personal and culturally determined. Venus and Serena are not beautiful by European standards. They are too dark, their features too clearly, absolutely non-White. But if I were to establish a "Black" standard of beauty, Venus and Serena Williams would symbolize it. We know how to articulate the beauty of light-skinned Black women, but what can we say of Venus and Serena?

I find their full lips and their substantial noses and their dark skin absolutely lovely. Not in some intellectual/theoretical way. I find their facial features lovely because they are full, fleshed out, absolute. The lips are made for smiling and perfectly match those noses. But Venus and Serena are also beautiful because they beam with an inner strength. When we look at darker-skinned women we may see them through a screen of darkness that renders them diminished the moment we gaze at them. A lighter-complexioned woman may appear full, complete, from the first glance. To look at a darker-skinned woman for many people is like looking at a photo in a half-lit room. The consciousness, the imagination, the brain, refuse to open to all that the face of a darker-skinned woman offers. All of these perceptions are the result of the culture that has given us the language we use to assess beauty, as well as the perspective that defines it.

Venus and Serena force us to confront and reassess our traditional notions of Black female beauty, the Black female body, and Black femininity. Close your eyes and think of the Black female body, the *brown to black female body*. This is the body we see bent over picking cotton, scarred by the lash of some overseer's whip, suckling a White baby at the dark, full breast; this is the body that has nappy hair, monkey lips; this is the body of "Mammy" and Aunt Jemima; the body of Sapphire, the body of Beulah, of Geraldine, the femme fatale of comedian Flip Wilson's weekly show in the 1970s; this is the body of Sheniqua, the neck-rolling, eye-popping, finger-snapping ghetto sister;

the body of Shenehneh, comedian Martin Lawrence's female alter ego in the 1990s; head rag–wearing domestic workers, welfare mothers, pregnant teenaged girls; those are the images we associate with brown to black women, and these are the words: mannish, sassy, big-mouthed, hard, asexual, tough, *full of attitude*.

But Venus and Serena are two dark-skinned Black women who are sexy, smart, ambitious, disciplined, confident, successful, beautiful women who have established their own fashion identity, who have endured the racism of the tennis world and the jealousy they have encountered with no public tantrums and with a nearly old-fashioned, ladylike grace. They are young women who have talked about their religious faith, their family, wanting to have a life *after* tennis, and who seem to always (in public, anyway) keep their eyes on the sparrow and on the prize. Venus and Serena are *our* girls next door. And in this public presentation of themselves they are an antidote to the more typical public imagery that defines and afflicts brown to black women. Black comedians and filmmakers, songwriters, purveyors of popular culture, and even some Black creators of "high" Black culture work assiduously to keep the more traditional perceptions alive.

But the creation and manipulation of body and sexual and female imagery has become an act that Serena, the younger sister, performs as consciously and adroitly as she rules the tennis court. Serena is compact, muscular, built for the game she dominates. And any discussion of Serena

Williams has to begin with her backside, her Black, her African, derriere. That's my backside, that's the backside of so many Black women, and Serena ain't trying to hide it, camouflage it, or do anything but flaunt it. If Serena Williams had done nothing more in her manipulation of Black female body image than appear on the court during the 2002 U.S. Open tennis championship wearing a short, form-fitting black Lycra jumpsuit that emphasized the beauty and prominence of her booty, she would have done enough.

I remember growing up feeling ashamed of my hips and buying clothes a size larger to try to hide them. I remember obsessing about *my ass*, constantly measuring it with a tape and never being satisfied with what the tape told me. I remember hours and hours spent exercising so I could have a White girl's ass instead. Serena exults in *her* ass, rejoicing in her generous backside. All this in-your-face celebration of her body liberates me, and it serves somehow to rescue and reclaim and reshape the tragic memory of the Venus Hottentot, a South African woman of generous physical proportions who was displayed in a cage throughout Europe in the late 1880s as an example of the "African species."

The Black female body has been owned, created, dissected, inspected, and presented historically by everyone but Black females, and our anatomy, our African-inherited anatomy, has become the object of derision and shame. Serena put on her jumpsuit and declared her black body sexy, athletic, and attractive. Serena lives inside her Black female body with a comfort that is unusual and refreshing. It is important to understand that Serena Williams is by her public presentation asserting that brown to black women are sexual, and feminine. And because Serena has achieved greatness and notoriety in the world of athletics, and *not* entertainment, this assertion is all the more potent.

P*latinum blonde. Golden blonde. Trophy blonde. Beautiful blonde. Dumb blonde. Gentlemen prefer blondes.*

Half of all the women in the U.S. color their hair with 40% opting for blonde. A 1991 study found 80% of American boys prefer blondes to brunettes or redheads.
—U.S. NEWS AND WORLD REPORT

I've been absolutely fascinated by the subject [of blondness] for years. As an Italian American I have to say that blondness has been one of the most oppressive themes of my entire life! My Italian immigrant family were aliens in upstate New York, which was still very conservative and Protestant. These local pressures were reinforced by the national messages about blondes coming from ads and the media. . . . By the time I reached adolescence, I conceded the superiority—might I say, the metaphysical superiority— of blondness. This was in high school where the social set was ruled by the blonde sorority queens and where I totally

accepted their master-race domination. Their social tyranny
seemed to me based in the undeniable reality of their
beauty. . . . So even though I knew I was infinitely
smarter than the blondes and much more talented,
I still was awed by them and viewed them
as Olympian goddesses.
. . . It's beyond ethics, it's beyond good and evil, this
reaction that people have to blondes. . . .
I had a blonde girlfriend, and it was just amazing to walk
down the street with her. I had never realized the way
people go mad for blondes. We would be walking along,
and the cars would start honking, and strangers would
call out to her, and it was just like the whole world
fell down at her feet.

—CAMILLE PAGLIA, *INTERVIEW* MAGAZINE

Guys always cheated on me with women who were
European-looking. You know, the long hair type. . . .
Being a regular Black girl wasn't good enough.

—LIL' KIM, *NEWSWEEK* MAGAZINE

Sheila: When you have good hair, of course you're happy
about it and you feel special and more privileged than
those who don't have good hair. People who don't have
good hair are envious of those who do. So, yeah, it's
very, very, very, very, important.

—FROM *HAIR MATTERS: BEAUTY, POWER, AND*
BLACK WOMEN'S CONSCIOUSNESS
BY INGRID BANKS

*Black women spend more money than any other group
on their hair, go through more anguish, and they
seem to have less success with it.*

—BARRY FLETCHER, HAIRDRESSER AND
AUTHOR OF *WHY ARE BLACK WOMEN
LOSING THEIR HAIR?*

I am in the grocery store, standing in line at the cashier, when I see Serena Williams on the cover of *Ebony*. In the color photograph, she manages to be so many things— svelte, voluptuous, and muscular in a form-fitting hot pink gown with a plunging neckline that exposes a hint of breast. Diamond bracelets sparkle on her wrists, and her oval face is framed by blond tresses that lie like airbrushed feathers against her shoulders and dip into her décolletage. Serena is smiling, a thousand-watt, ten-million-dollar smile.

I reach for the magazine, a near tumult of emotions fomenting inside me. Her body is buff and beautiful, but the sight of the blond tresses, the weave so deftly done that it completely obscures her own hair, fills me with ambivalence. Serena is smiling like a little girl playing dress-up before the mirror in expensive clothes that belong to her mother. She is smiling with a satisfaction that I want to believe is generated by her accomplishments and her inner sense of worth, and not by the fact that she resembles a Black blond version of Madonna.

The texture and the length of hair is as much a part of the color complex as is skin tone. Hair is political, sociological, and can be, although it is not always, a barometer of a person's state of mind. I wore my hair permed for several years while living in Nigeria, and the permanent had no effect on my politics or sense of identity. But Black women are fired, demoted, reprimanded, and ostracized for wearing locks, twists, or braids in some workplaces because the look is "too ethnic." Black men and women still often choose their mates to ensure that their offspring will have "good hair." The Afro was a symbol of the rejection of White definitions of beauty and an assertion of racial pride. Long blond hair is the stuff of fairy tales and myths and legends and is one of the most enduring and potent symbols of beauty in our culture. In twenty-five years of teaching at historically White colleges, I have had numerous conversations with White female students about the double standard among Whites that privileges the "all-American" girl with blond hair and blue eyes. My female students spoke with as much pain and anguish about intraracial discrimination among Whites as Black women have evidenced in discussions about *our* color complex. I had thought the blond hair fetish was an artificial, manufactured reality, but my female students informed me that it was real and that it affected the way that they were perceived and how much they were valued by family, men, and employers.

Hair is not an academic matter. It is controversial, emotional, a source of pride or loathing, and it is the easiest and most economical alteration that a woman can make in her appearance and in her presentation to the world. And when it comes to hair color, blond is the most loaded color of all.

I buy the issue of *Ebony* with Serena on the cover, the headline promising, *"Serena as you have never seen her before."* At home I read the article, which is mostly a boisterous declaration of independence, an assertion that Serena is "little sister" no more. She is having the time of her life in these photos. There is the sultry Serena, in Victoria's Secret–style panties and bra, draped in a sheer, see-through black fitted caftan; there is the almost inno-cent Serena in tight jeans and a leather fringed top; there is the relaxed Serena, hugging her pet pit bull, wearing a halter top and slacks, her blond hair half braided, half free-flowing. In the article, Serena reveals that in her life after tennis she wants to become an actress. This, I feel, in part explains the blond hair. Women who want to in-tensify their sexuality and femininity and who want to heighten their sense of female power often become blondes. And blond is the ultimate color for female film stars and sex symbols. Women sometimes become blondes to will themselves into success and to reward themselves for achieving their dreams. *Serena is African American, but probably asks herself, "Why should White girls have all the fun?"*

I experience such an awful mess of responses as I turn the pages and Serena's smile beams out at me like a laser boring into my heart. And what I feel is all about her hair.

My husband tells me that "for the young folks today blond is just a color, and that's as it should be." Feminist critics of popular culture write that blond Lil' Kim and Mary J. Blige are cultural rebels redefining the stereotype of the hyper-sexed Black woman, courageously making it their own by relocating it in the model of the dominant culture. *One negative stereotype within another negative stereotype*, it's just that this time we control it. *Okay*.

Freedom is a conundrum and a treasure, and it is neither neat nor logical. As I gaze at Serena, I am thrust back in front of my childhood mirror, the one I finally broke. I look at Serena and I am ten years old again with scarves pinned to my head. This is my problem, not Serena's, but Serena and all my sisters become blond within a frame-work of continuing and persistent self-hatred among African Americans that simply can't be denied.

Hair is history. Hair is religion. Hair is politics. And blondness is many things for a Black woman. It is whimsy. It is a fashion statement. It is a fad. It's a puzzle. It is a question. Does a sister look in the mirror at her blond hair and think, *Free at last?* A friend who lives in Atlanta tells me that she attended a party and when she walked in, "half the people there were huddled in a corner talking about Serena Williams's blond hair." This same friend and I talk about Serena as a manifestation of the "ghetto fabulous" syndrome—gold teeth, gold chains, pet pit bulls, ostenta-tious displays of fashion style designed to make a statement about wealth (real or imagined)—and Serena's adherence to some of the symbols of that norm. But blond hair and weaves and extensions that reach to a woman's backside are no longer just a fashion statement in the ghetto but have become a part of mainstream Black female style and expression.

I finally admit that because Serena is dark-skinned I find the blond hair incongruous. I admit that while I applaud what Serena is saying with her body, there is a part of me that wants to censor the statement I read into her hair. But therein lies the hypocrisy. Therein lies the corrupted vision. Therein lies the evidence of my own color complex. Serena is too dark to be a blonde because that is the vision, the tunnel vision, I have inherited from decades of colorist and racist conditioning. Serena has liberated *me*, but I still want to keep *her* in jail.

The times, they are a'changin'. White youth, en masse, adopt the fashion styles of Blacks—baggy pants, dreadlocks, even the ghetto pimp swagger. And there is a flagrant, nearly joyous meshing and fusing of styles among young people today that throws everything up for question, from sexual identity and preference to racial designation and even the significance of race. This is freedom of a sort. It is a freedom panting and scratching for life within the borders of a society and culture that is "mulatto" "melting pot" "stewed" "omni-American" brown, neither White nor Black, but a culture that remains one in which African

Americans are economically and politically influential but bereft of meaningful power in either sphere, and where Black beauty is still a concept up for grabs.

I find the boldness with which pockets of the White and Black communities are wide open to reimagining themselves without the straitjacketing strictures of the past exhilarating and heartening. But my excitement does not blind me to the persistence of the rules of the race and color-complex game.

Some Black girls still look in the mirror and want to be White. Whether they want to look like Angelina Jolie or a light-skinned video ho, what they don't want to be is their brown to black, darker-skinned selves. And in our community even the youngest girls feel the pressure to have long hair, be it braided, woven, extended, or straightened. While all of these are viable options for hair care, we telegraph to our daughters very early on that they do not have to accept or love their short hair, their coarse hair, and that the Afro, the natural (and all that it symbolizes), is a thing of the past.

During a visit to the Harry Winston jeweler on Fifth Avenue in New York, Serena met with three little African American girls who were participants in the Fresh Air Fund, a charity that provides underprivileged New York children with summer vacations in the country. Blond Serena autographed the girls' T-shirts and posed for pictures with them. While Serena was being interviewed by reporters, the little girls stood giddy and awed, giggling and gazing at Serena with youthful admiration and envy. According to a *Washington Post* article that captured the vignette, the girls were riveted mostly by Serena's blond tresses and were overheard to say repeatedly, "Man, she has nice hair."

Far from Home

The black woman has no place in the
established canon of beauty.
—ELVIRA CERVERA, CUBAN ACTRESS

The blood of Africa runs deep in our veins.
—FIDEL CASTRO

The problem of the twentieth century is the problem
of the colorline, the relation of the darker
to the lighter races of men.
—W. E. B. DUBOIS

I t is 1977 and I am living in Lagos, Nigeria, with my
Nigerian first husband, Femi, whom I met while he was
studying at Cornell University. Nigeria is a sprawling,
populous country, one of the largest on the African continent. I am living there in the midst of the country's oil
boom, a time of military rule and feeble, halfhearted attempts at economic and social progress. Mandating ele-
mentary school education as a requirement for all children

and building better roads and superhighways barely begin to address the gargantuan problems of this nation of 100 million people and 250 languages. The illiteracy rate is 70 percent, telephones rarely work, much of the country lacks electricity, and power shortages and blackouts are epidemic. The capital city, Lagos, is filthy and overcrowded, and known internationally for its infamous "go-slow"—hydra-headed traffic jams in which cars, from Mercedes-Benzes and Hondas to vans, trucks, and lorries creep at an agonizing pace of three, four, five hours to get from one end of the island to the other.

Yet for all its problems, Nigeria has a population that is aggressive, resilient, and hardworking. The country is respected for its oil (it is the second largest exporter of oil to the United States) and for its often progressive stance in international and African affairs (providing material support to the antiapartheid movement and helping to create ECOWAS, the Economic Community of West African States). Nigerian musicians, from King Sunny Ade to Fela Ransome Kuti, have created a style of music that has put the country on the international pop culture map. And the country wields enormous political and social influence on the continent.

It is 1977, and though Nigeria is free of British colonial rule it is being invaded and colonized once again. This time the culprit is neocolonialism, a system of international businesses working closely with wealthy Nigerians to create an economy largely dependent on the West (Europe and America) for everything from food to cars to clothing, as well as the exploitation of the country's substantial raw materials. It is 1977, and American culture, its music, films, magazines, television, and fashion, have become a major shaper of public tastes, desires, and the consciousness of youth. This in a country where polygamy and genital mutilation are still widely practiced.

I have lived in Nigeria for two years. I teach mass communication and journalism at the University of Lagos, where most of my students are male and many of my colleagues are "been-tos"—Nigerians who have "been to," in the popular vernacular, America or Britain to study for university degrees and who have returned to teach in the country's still growing network of colleges and universities. By marriage, I am part of a prosperous Yoruba clan. My husband's father, who died the year before, had twelve wives and had sired nearly sixty children. The status of members of Femi's family ranges from Ph.D.s to the illiterate, from business tycoons to the wretchedly poor. The Ajayi women, as is the custom among the Yoruba, are industrious and independent, often working as market women and entrepreneurs who control their own money, honor the complex and intricate obligations that bind them to family, and allow their husbands to think that it is they who are fully in charge of everything.

Femi is tall, ebony black, and proud. He pursued me, while I was enrolled in graduate school at Columbia, with an enticing mix of humility and eagerness. I fell in love with him in part because of what he symbolized, not just Africa but extended, active family ties. But living in

Nigeria, I have wrestled with a daunting mix of frustration (at the country's underdevelopment and the blatant sexism of the culture) and pride (I love living in a country where everyone looks like me, and as an educated American, even an American woman, I have been offered impressive professional opportunities). I have learned to speak Yoruba, eat and enjoy Nigerian dishes like pounded yam and moi moi, and respect the culture's reverence for the elderly.

I watch with fascination and excitement as hundreds of African Americans arrive in Lagos for the international Black arts and culture festival FESTAC. Stuck in the interminable go-slow, I can turn on the radio in my Subaru and hear Stevie Wonder's "I Wish," or Bill Withers's "Lovely Day." The deejay will hold forth in a mix of Nigerian vernacular and Black American–influenced slang. Young Nigerian girls wear cornrows and braids and are beginning to get their hair permed. And I watch in horror as what Nigerians come to call "yellow fever"—the use of skin-lightening creams—spreads across the country like a modern-day plague.

Yinka's Story

She is light but wants to be lighter still. Yinka, my husband's cousin, is a twenty-year-old student majoring in math at the University of Ibadan. She sits in our living room this Sunday afternoon, updating Femi and me and

Femi's brother Jide and his wife, Ayo, about her studies, her part-time job, and the health and welfare of members of the clan who live in Ibadan. Yinka is an ebullient, cheerful young woman whom I have met at various family occasions. Her hair is neatly cornrowed and she is dressed in a Calvin Klein jean skirt and white blouse. She sits demurely, sipping an orange Fanta, meeting the puzzled, shamed stare of her family with a staunch gaze.

Her light brown complexion has been ravaged. Her skin is raw, as though diseased, and deep pockmarks are embedded in her cheeks. Her face is much lighter than her neck and arms—evidence of the bleaching creams she has been using. Femi, Jide, Ayo, normally boisterous, gregarious conversationalists, especially with kin, sit mute at the sight of Yinka. It has been months since we have seen her, and she sits chattering despite the uncomfortable silence, clearly proud of her new shade of skin. I sit in abject, total amazement, for it is clear that like more and more Nigerians, Yinka is not merely using bleaching creams, she is misusing them. I have seen the creams, Nadinola, Ambi, and others, in the local pharmacies and in stalls in the open markets. The creams are imported from the United States. I was surprised and dismayed when I first saw them on the shelves of stores and stacked beside yams, plantains, and cloth in the marketplace. *Another romantic illusion of Africa shot down,* I thought.

Then I began to see, or rather, to admit to my resisting mind that I was seeing, the bleachers, so many of them that singer and songwriter Fela Ransome Kuti, a folk hero and political activist, recorded a hit song called "Yellow Fever" deriding the craze. The song is popular, but it has not stopped the purchase and use of the creams. I see the bleachers, men and women, young and middle aged, on the streets of Lagos. I see them wearing traditional Nigerian dress and Western-style business suits. I see them and feel shame at their lack of racial pride, resentment that they are imitating the worst of African American habits, and I fear for their health. In the America I left behind, the use of skin lighteners has plummeted since the sixties. I find myself living in one of the major African nations amid a generation of young people entranced with lightness and whiteness, men and women who use the creams with a dedication that is mind-boggling. I have talked with other American wives who tell me that Nigerians apply the creams over their entire bodies, use much more than the recommended dosage, and use the creams for much longer than is safe.

The bleaching creams contain hydroquinone, a carcinogen that breaks down melanin. It is melanin that makes us brown to black. It is melanin that protects people of African descent from the sun's radiation. Some of the creams even contain steroids. By weakening the melanin-producing cells in the skin, the creams make the users vulnerable to skin cancer.

When Yinka leaves, Jide shouts in disgust, "That foolish girl. Why does she want to do that? She's killing herself." Later that evening, Femi is too upset to talk with me about Yinka. He is upset, and I can also tell that he is

ashamed that I have witnessed this level of racial confusion and self-hatred in a member of his family. When we
were in America, Femi told me that he was going to bring
me "home" to live in Nigeria. He is a man of enormous
pride, in himself and in his ethnic and racial heritage. I
know that it hurts him deeply that his wife, a descendant
of Africa whose original progenitors may have been stolen
from some village within the borders of Nigeria, has returned "home" to see Yinka's confusion and self-loathing.

Africans brought to America were enslaved physically
and mentally. In Africa, colonization taught Africans that
their culture, religion, and traditions were worthless and
backward, that civilization was "brought" to the continent
by Europeans, and that the Black African body was ugly
and an object of degradation. I came to Nigeria naively believing and secretly hoping that the pride I witnessed in
Femi and his friends and family in America was the norm.
I found my African brothers and sisters shouldering the
same psychological burdens that I was so familiar with
from my life in the United States.

I know that the invasion of European and American
films and television programs, with their exaltation of
White female beauty, White male heroism, White economic and social power, White life, and, by extension,
White skin, are only part of the problem. Mass media is an
intoxicating drug, a potent form of propaganda. But this
ongoing cultural narrative has interacted with African
minds poisoned by generations of "psychological colonialism" and shame among some at many things African. Over

dinner one night a friend of Femi's, who like Femi is a
"been-to," insisted to me that the images of African
women with their breasts uncovered that were often featured in the pages of *National Geographic* bore no relation
to anything he had ever seen growing up in his village.
"The women in Ijero never walked around like that. They
must have paid those women to bare their breasts," he argued, puffing in agitation on his pipe. But I had seen older
women sitting outside their small houses in Femi's home
village, their empty, sagging breasts uncovered as they
sucked on a chewing stick or gnawed on a kola nut. After
Bola departed, Femi shook his head and laughed. "Don't
mind him, he just cares too much what the Whites think
about us. You will see his own mother, her breasts bared, if
you go to Ijero today. We were never ashamed of naked-
ness until the Whites told us to be."

I am aware of the colorist impulse among Nigerians but
have chosen, until Yinka's visit, to ignore it. But when my
cousin Debra spends several weeks with me during her
summer vacation I notice how the men in Femi's family are
enthralled by her light complexion, and how they virtually
camp out at our house while she is there. Femi's younger
brothers compete to bring her gifts, to take her to see the
sights of Lagos, and I watch them gaze approvingly at her
and speak openly of how pretty she is because she is
"bright"—light in complexion.

When my son is born two years later, my mother-in-
law beams at the sight of him in his first weeks, smiling
broadly as she concludes, *"O lewa pupa,"* roughly trans-

lated as "how pretty," because of his light brown complexion. She has come, as custom requires, to spend several weeks with me after the birth of our son, and as Michael's skin tone changes to brown, my mother-in-law becomes disgruntled and disapproving. She loves her grandson but had just hoped that his light skin was permanent.

I want to talk to Yinka, to ask her why she bleaches. Despite her nonchalant air during her visit, I know that she must be self-conscious and sensitive about the subject. I am sure that she knows as well that the Ajayi clan is abuzz with gossip and recrimination about her use of skin lighteners. Because I cannot talk to Yinka, I talk instead to two of my female students, one a Yoruba, Bisi, and the other an Igbo, Buchi. Bisi wants to be a reporter for Nigeria's national television news network. Buchi dreams of reporting on Africa for the BBC.

The two young women are willing and even eager to talk with me about the subject, and Bisi has written an article on bleaching for the student newspaper. "Why?" I ask, looking at the two attractive young women across the desk in my small office on campus.

"The girls want to be pretty, and they think being pretty means having lighter skin," Bisi tells me. "They listen to the boys who say that light is better and in order to get the boys, they use the creams."

Buchi adds, "The boys are so hypocritical. On the one hand they criticize the girls for using the creams, saying they are not really natural women, not African, but though they say that they often chase after the bleachers anyway."

When I ask how important the attitudes of men are in determining whether a women will use skin lighteners, both Buchi and Bisi say that it's a crucial factor.

"It's not like in America," Bisi tells me, "where a woman can be single, where she can be unmarried and do what she wants, live any type of life she desires."

"In Nigeria," Buchi cuts in, "we have no concept of a woman being single, surely not choosing to be single anyway. A woman has to be married. She has to have a husband and children or she isn't a real woman. So some of the girls will do anything they think will get them a man."

In an hourlong conversation I begin to gain a deeper sense of the forces that encourage the use of the bleaching creams. Both young women tell me that, as I suspected, bleaching is mostly an urban rather than a rural phenomenon. "In the village they would be beaten with sticks," Bisi says with a harsh laugh. "People would be afraid that they were ghosts." The use of the bleaching creams is also, both women tell me, part of the overall urbanization, modernization, and Westernization of the country.

"Anybody who wants an education, who wants to make money, comes to Lagos, Ibadan, or Port Harcourt," Buchi explains. "And everybody, no matter how backward or illiterate, once they come to the city, wants to be associated with what they see on television, in the glossy magazines, and in the movies."

Young women with education want to marry a "been-to" or become one. Young men with ambition often want to study in Britain or America and return with a foreign wife, who in the eyes of their friends will be viewed as a trophy brought back from the Promised Land. Clothing from America can be sold for hundreds of dollars, and to be hip, to be "in," is to eat and enjoy American hamburgers *and* gari. For women, being attractive increasingly means looking Western, looking American. Everyone on the move wants to leave his or her village roots behind. Bisi and Buchi tell me that lighter skin is associated even among Nigerians with a host of positive attributes, from beauty to wealth to intelligence.

"I have to tell you, I never expected to see anything like this when I came here," I tell the two young women in exasperation. "In America I could understand this. I feel like all the books I read about African history and politics told me only part of the story. I understand this in America. We were enslaved."

"We are the slaves now," Bisi says grimly with pursed lips. "We are the slaves now."

Women in Africa are economically dependent on men. . . . Women need men in their lives to survive. If the general view is that light-skinned women are more attractive, then it's an investment to try to lighten one's skin. They are not just buying cream. They are buying a dream of a better life.

—IRENE NJOROGE, A KENYAN COSMETOLOGIST AND ANTIBLEACHING ACTIVIST

Throughout Latin America's countrysides, from Guatemala
to Costa Rica, from Venezuela to Paraguay, the same
stark pigmentocratic reality holds. Tall, light-skinned,
Voltaire-steeped owners of latifundios *dominate—and*
in many cases browbeat and brutalize through private
militias—the vastly more numerous, shorter, darker
Indian-featured peasants who labor for them, usually
barefoot, alongside children whose bellies
are bloated with parasites.

—FROM *WORLD ON FIRE* BY AMY CHUA

Skin bleaching and lightening have reached epidemic proportions throughout Africa, the Caribbean, Latin America, and even in Asia. In Jamaica it's called "browning." The creams and lotions, now imported mostly from Europe rather than America, have caused so many health problems that governments in Nigeria, Uganda, Kenya, and Zambia have banned or cracked down on the importation and sale of skin lighteners. But the products remain easy to purchase on the black market and are extremely popular.

People of color all over the world, Africans, Asians, Indians, use skin lighteners and believe that their lives will be improved if their skin is lighter. Everything that they see in their societies supports this belief. I have traveled widely throughout the Caribbean islands, and the darker-skinned people are always performing the most menial tasks and live in the most impoverished conditions. Turn on the television in any country of brown to black people from Brazil to India and you would think there are no darker-hued people in the country. People who lighten their skin are not crazy. They know what they see. They know how the world works. Light skin equals privilege, power, and influence. The youngest person in the ghettos of Port-au-Prince, Kingston, or Trinidad can see that. It is useless to criticize darker-skinned people for using skin creams unless a world is created where Blackness is loved and revered. Talk of racial pride, dignity, and self-respect seems a callous insult and makes no sense in the world in which most people of color live. In underdeveloped countries where a college education, with its promise of upward mobility and success, is an out-of-reach fantasy for most people, skin lighteners are a cheap and easily obtainable alternative, a fast but hardly painless way to attain "beauty" and status. The Black Consciousness and Black Pride Movements of the sixties and seventies were an outgrowth and a component of intense political and social reform movements that sought to and indeed did change society. Banning the creams may perhaps save the skins of Black people, but much more is needed to save their minds and their lives.

From "Globalization of Beauty Makes Slimness Trendy" in the *New York Times*, October 3, 2002:

Lagos, Nigeria—With no success, Nigeria had been sending contestants to the Miss World pageant for years. Winners of the Most Beautiful Girl in Nigeria went year after year to the Miss World competition, and year after year the beauty queens performed poorly.

Guy Murray-Bruce, the executive director of Silverbird Productions, which runs the Most Beautiful Girl contest, said he had almost resigned himself to the fact that black African women had little chance of winning an international competition in a world dominated by Western beauty ideals.

Then in 2000 he carried out a drastic change of strategy in picking the Most Beautiful Girl and Nigeria's next international representative.

"The judges had always looked for a local queen, someone they considered a beautiful African woman," Mr. Murray-Bruce, 38, said. "So I told the judges not to look for a local queen, but someone to represent us internationally."

The new strategy's success was immediate. The Most Beautiful Girl of 2001, Agbani Darego, went on to clinch the Miss World title in Sun City, South Africa, last October. She became the first African winner in the contest's 51-year history [emphasis mine].

Her victory stunned Nigerians, whose country had earned a worldwide reputation for corruption and fraud. Now, all of a sudden, Nigeria was No. 1 in beautiful

women. Mrs. Darego, who was 18 at the time, instantly
became a national heroine.

But soon pride gave way to puzzlement. In a culture
where Coca-Cola bottle voluptuousness is celebrated and
ample backsides and bosoms are considered ideals of
female beauty, the new Miss World shared none of those
attributes. She was 6 feet tall, stately, and so, so skinny.
She was, some said uncharitably, a white girl in black
skin.

. . .

The change is an example of the power of Western
culture on a continent caught between tradition and
modernity. Older Nigerians' views of beauty have not
changed, but among young, fashionable Nigerians,
voluptuousness is out and thin is in.

It is 1984, and I have been divorced from Femi for six
years. Simmering emotional incompatibilities finally led
to a separation and divorce. I am back home in the States,
and after living in Boston for several years and ever goaded
by the need for adventure and afflicted with a perennial
wanderlust, I spend three weeks in Senegal, where I meet
Marc, a Belgian painter, and embark on an intense, passionate affair that lasts a year and during which I live with
him in Belgium and Paris.

Several weeks after my return to Boston from Senegal,
Marc commits a grand romantic gesture that is ironic,

shamelessly sentimental, and enormously gratifying to me. When I arrive home one afternoon I find a note from the front office asking me to retrieve a large package. I live in a former piano factory that has been turned into loft living/working space for the city's arts community. When I go to the front office I see a large four-by-five-foot cardboard container. My next-door neighbor, artist Paul Goodnight, helps me bring the cardboard box to my apartment, and he opens it while grilling me, unconvinced by my assertions that I have no idea what this package contains.

Inside we find two large silkscreens that Marc has made and sent to me as an homage to our time together in Dakar. One silkscreen is of Leopold Senghor, the great poet and prophet of Negritude; the other a photo of me blown up to proportions that fill half the large canvas, surrounded by mementos of our time together—an article from the Dakar newspaper published on the day we met, a ticket stub from a boat ride to Goree Island to see the slave castle, lines from a note I left for Marc at the front desk of his hotel. I stand nearly paralyzed by surprise and joy. Paul Goodnight laughs and says, "I think it's safe to say this man is in love."

Marc tells me early in our relationship that I am beautiful and that he is attracted to women of color because of the beauty of our skin, because we have color. He has grown up in a country of what he calls "wretchedly pale people," and he finds all the shades that Black people possess, from café au lait to ebony, "a gift from God."

No one has ever spoken to me about color, my color, in this way, and during my time in Belgium and Paris, I am heady with a heightened sense of my allure. I had hungered for adventure and I found it. Eager to spend more time writing, I quit my teaching position at Emerson College and join Marc in Europe. My son, Michael, is cared for by friends for several weeks while Marc and I decide where we will live. I dive headlong into this new life. Friends have met Marc during a monthlong visit he made to Boston and find him as irresistible as I do, but still they caution me not to burn all my bridges.

Paris is where writers James Baldwin and Richard Wright lived in exile and found a refuge and respite from American racism. It is a city that since the late 1880s has attracted Black Americans seeking opportunities denied them in America. Like those Black people who preceded me, I too feel freer and less racially oppressed in the City of Lights. I feel freed of the burden of both racism and colorism. Walking the streets of Paris with Marc, I recall the French fascination with African American singer Josephine Baker in the twenties, how she became the tan empress of Paris, the toast of the town. I am aware of the European fascination with black and brown women as the "Other," as sexual and exotic because of our African origins. But I am also aware of how right I feel inside my skin in France and Belgium, where my race seems to matter little and my relationship with Marc attracts no public attention at all.

I probe myself often during this affair, wondering at the complexity of racial desire. If a Black man expressed a fascination with and preference for White women I would go ballistic, assuming that his feelings were inevitably tied to and had sprung from self-hatred. Marc, however, as a White male, even as a visual artist of modest means, can walk the streets of Dakar or Paris with equal ease, his Whiteness the source of his power and privilege, certainly not a thing he would wish to deny or seek to escape. His attraction to Black women exists alongside his confidence in and acceptance of the validity of his European heritage and his white skin. I had heard even before coming to Europe that some European men really did believe "the blacker the berry, the sweeter the juice."

Writer Audrey Edwards has written, "The first man to ever tell me I was beautiful was white." She has also concluded that "familiarity does perhaps in-breed contempt for men and women of like race. Opposites do, in fact, probably attract if left unencumbered by the weight of history and stereotype."

Back home and even abroad, I know that my African American brothers are more likely to rhapsodize over a Black woman who is light-skinned. I have heard them. I have seen them turn into putty, Jell-O, fools, clowns, all to get the attention of a light-skinned sister. My lover, a European, not only tells me my brown skin is lovely but fills several large canvases with silkscreens and collages of my brown face.

A few of my friends are shocked that I am involved with a White man, and a Belgian at that. They remind me of the atrocities and the horrors the Belgians inflicted on the Congo during the decades of their bloody colonial rule.

I tell them that Marc wasn't even born then, that he has traveled widely in Africa, worked with an international organization that encouraged cultural exchange between European and African artists, and that our political views are virtually identical. Marc has seen the beauty that I know I possess and is willing to articulate it, to codify it and make it special and sacred in images and words. That feels good. It feels damn good. But all of that isn't enough to build a mature relationship on, and when Marc and I are tested in the aftermath of the initial glow of infatuation, we fail each other. And I discover that for Marc, like Femi, emotional intimacy is difficult to achieve and sustain.

Of course, we suffer the same self-hatred in Sudan. We worship the Arabs and hate our Black skin, but it's still not as bad as it is here in America. I really had a hard time adjusting, because most Black Americans are so used to self-hating non-African society that they don't even notice how toxic their lives and communities are.

—KOLA BOOF

When in 1990 I meet Joe Murray, the man I will ultimately marry and come to view not only as a husband but as a life partner and friend, I am impressed that he, like me, has traveled widely and has a broad international perspective on life, living, and politics. Joe's country of choice, or, rather, his addiction, is Brazil, which he has visited seven times. He's drawn to the country because of its large Black population and because, he says, "In a way it's like America, but every city is like a different country." In the first weeks of dating we trade notes about our international journeys. He speaks fondly of time spent in São Paolo, Rio de Janeiro, Bahia, and other Brazilian cities.

I have learned snippets of information about the country. Most of what I know revolves around the complex notions of race. I know that Brazil is a largely Black and mulatto nation, one in which dark-skinned Blacks with straight hair and keen features who are middle class or affluent can define themselves as White and no one blinks an eye. They "earn" the blessing of whiteness and overcome the blight of blackness through hard work and success. I know that the country has created a mythology that it is the racial land of milk and honey, but that a nascent Black Consciousness Movement is taking hold among Black Brazilians.

Early on Joe shared an anecdote with me that he tells frequently as a commentary about color in Brazil.

"When I started going to Brazil, I would go with the names and addresses and phone numbers of Brazilians from all walks of life who had been my pen pals. I'd call and try to make a date for us to get together. I wanted of course to see the sights of whatever city I was in, but mostly I wanted to meet Brazilians, the real people, who could educate me about the culture and the people just by being with them. Normally what would happen is that I would get a quick return call from the light Brazilians and we would go to dinner, to clubs, to museums. Over and over, the dark Brazilians either didn't return my calls at all or by the time they did get in touch with me I was ready to return home. I have to admit that I was pretty pissed, figuring that the darker-skinned Brazilians were trifling, or maybe even had something against African Americans. Then on one trip I finally hooked up with a dark-skinned Brazilian woman who was referred to me by a friend in D.C. I visited her, and when she told me about her life, I finally understood. She, like so many of the dark-skinned Brazilians, lived in a poorer neighborhood, and she worked as a maid during the day. Then she had a second job at night. She somehow managed to squeeze me in between her jobs, and I told her how frustrated I was by the response of Black Brazilians, the people I really wanted to meet and get to know. But when she told me about her life and the life of her friends and family I understood that color was really important in Brazil. The lighter-skinned Brazilians had more free time to spend with me, more money because they worked at good jobs and didn't have to work two and three jobs to make ends meet. All the darker-skinned Brazilians I ultimately met were so busy struggling to survive that they had no time to go with me to a museum and little money to go to dinner or a club. So when I hear people come back from Brazil talking about how there's no racism, I tell them what I know."

Journalist Eugene Robinson writes that during his time in Brazil he found that "there were literally dozens of terms for skin color—black, white, mulatto and *pardo*, of course, but also more fanciful and evocative terms. In surveys, Brazilians have described themselves or others as 'burned,' 'burned by the sun,' 'around midnight,' 'after midnight,' 'chocolate,' 'coffee with milk,' and 'navy blue.' One particularly subtle and elusive hue was called 'miscegenation.' "

From the beginning of history the concept of blackness was very very different. In Egypt they called themselves the Black people, and Kemit, the original name of Egypt, means "The land of the Black people." In the ancient Congo they took so much pride in being Black, the blacker the child was the better. They put babies in the sun to become darker. But today there is nearly universal condemnation of blackness.

—HISTORIAN RUNOKO RASHIDI

Joe and I visit Cuba for a week in the spring of 2002 with a group of educators from Washington, D.C., who work in the field of adult literacy. The group has come to Cuba to meet with their counterparts, to exchange ideas, success stories, and challenges. This small island has a literacy rate of nearly 100 percent, higher than that of the United States and many other industrial nations. Cuba regularly sends cadres of adult literacy experts to other Caribbean countries and to Latin and Central America to assist in eradicating illiteracy, which remains a scourge of many developing nations. Cuba essentially wrote the book on how to turn a largely illiterate country into a nation that can read, and this group of educators is here to learn how they did it.

My political sympathies are with the socialist revolution that changed everything in the country in 1959. For most of my adult life I have avidly followed the progress of the Revolution, and I know that Cuba's social-safety-net-guaranteed housing, jobs, free education, and health care have placed the country in the forefront of governments that can be called socially progressive. This has been accomplished in the shadow of a U.S. embargo on trade that has soured U.S.-Cuba relations and undeniably crippled the lives of millions of Cubans, who have survived, nonetheless, on hard work, resilience, and imaginative responses to economic hardship. I was living in Nigeria when Castro sent Cuban troops to South Africa and Angola and helped the African freedom fighters in those countries win decisive victories. That act of Pan-Africanist support sealed Fidel Castro's image as a friend of African and Black people worldwide. I know that the Revolution dramatically changed the lives of Black Cubans (the majority of the population) for the better, ending legal discrimination and segregation and giving them a sense of long-denied dignity. But I have also heard from friends who have visited the island and I have read in reports that racial inequality remains a fact of life for Black Cubans and that the Revolution in that sense remains unfinished.

Before making the journey, I read several books on

Cuban history and learn among other things that under Spanish colonialism in Cuba, it was possible to buy a certificate that declared the race of a Black or mulatto person White. To ensure that his offspring became a person of privilege, a White father could swear that he did not know who the mother of his Black or mulatto child was, thereby purifying the child's blood, making it "White"; that Cuba was one of the last countries to abolish slavery, doing so in 1886; that the army that fought for Cuban independence from Spain was mostly Black; that in 1912, six thousand Black Cubans were massacred in what was called "The War of the Races"; and that the country is overwhelmingly "Black" with White Cubans outnumbered by mulattoes and Blacks two to one. I am going to Cuba to see not just the results of the Revolution but the faces of people whom history has made my brothers and sisters.

The city of Havana is both decrepit and lovely. The legacy of past splendor hangs over the city, reflected in the ornate centuries-old Spanish architecture of the municipal buildings. The housing stock throughout the island is old and largely has gone without repair for many years as the country prioritized the funding of social welfare programs. The streets are filled with lumbering, bulky, pollution-producing Chevrolets and Buicks from the 1950s, the long-ago era before the embargo. I have traveled throughout the developing world and am impressed with the cleanliness of Havana. There is no sense of overcrowding or a city straining under the weight of a sea of impoverished humanity.

Our guide is Manuel, an affable twenty-five-year-old Black Cuban. Manuel is dark-skinned and an articulate and eager college graduate at ease with our group of Americans. Most of us on the tour are African American, and we are openly pleased that we have a Black tour guide. From what I read before the trip I know that a job in the tourist industry is considered a high-status position. Even registering guests at the front desk and tending bar at a hotel are jobs that pay more than the meager though guaranteed salaries that most Cubans earn. As a tour guide, Manuel has a position that is prized, a job rarely held by a Black. With his excellent English, his friendly personality, his ability to put people at ease, his obvious intelligence, Joe and I conclude that Manuel must be a Cuban "super Black," who by dint of talent, drive, and ability takes advantage of openings in the system to become successful.

At the Literacy Museum we learn that after the Revolution, cadres of literate young people were sent into Cuba's poor rural provinces to teach the bulk of the island's population—mostly farm workers, to read. This was a war in a sense, one that produced young martyrs killed by opponents of Castro's ascension to power. Still, within a year, those who had been illiterate were able to read and write, most at a third-grade level. The final examination for all was to write a one-page letter to Castro. We were shown a letter written by a newly literate woman who wrote, "I never felt that I was Cuban until I learned to read." The literacy rate rose from 40 percent to nearly 100 percent. Before the Revolution, literacy was highest among White, urban Cubans.

Strolling through the streets of Old Havana, we pass historic buildings with exteriors painted in the most se-ductive and whimsical shades of blue, green, and pink. Old Havana is filled with cathedrals and is undergoing major renovation of buildings and restructuring as an enclave of restaurants and other tourist sites. We walk past buildings surrounded by stories-high scaffolding, the interiors dust-filled, construction workers busy with the tasks of renova-tion. There is a Benetton, several elegantly appointed eateries, flower shops, cafés, and sleek modern art galleries. As we are walking, Joe asks Manuel questions about his family, his interests, and then Joe asks Manuel who Cubans consider the symbol of female beauty. Manuel blushes and then laughs, and says, "A mulatto woman from the eastern part of Santiago de Cuba."

Our tour bus drives us one afternoon through a part of Havana with wide boulevards and parks. The large manor-like houses are now crumbling and in disrepair, but behind the wrought-iron fences and the palm trees leaning like sentries onto the roofs and shadowing vacant windows, the atmosphere of faded glory, luxury, and wealth nevertheless pervades the area like a muted perfume. The villas and mansions, which now house some embassies, restaurants, and private homes, are symbols of the ostentatious wealth that some on the island once possessed. This is where the landowners and industrialists lived. Manuel tells us that in the days before the Revolution, the only Black people allowed in this part of the city were those who worked as maids, drivers, nannies, and landscapers for the property owners. He also tells us that Fulgencio Batista, the military strongman overthrown by Castro's rebel forces, was a mulatto who even as head of state was not admitted to certain private clubs on the island because he was not White.

As our bus drives throughout the city, Manuel tells us that we should feel free to ask him anything we want about Cuba and that he will answer as honestly as he can.

"Does Castro have any Black people in his inner circle?" Joe shouts out, and before Manuel can answer he adds, "And I mean identifiably *black* people, not mulattoes." This is an important question for many of us on this trip, because the international face of the Revolution that we most often see is White—Castro, his brother Raoul, White Cubans lifted from rafts and rickety boats off the shore of Miami and guaranteed automatic asylum in the United States, Elian Gonzales, the boy whose custody sparked a near international incident. Where, we wonder, are Black Cubans in the public unfolding of the story of this country?

"There *are* Blacks in the upper echelons of government," Manuel assures us, giving us the names of the men and the positions they hold. However, Manuel does not dare touch the color issue and leaves part of my husband's question unanswered.

"Are they in the inner circle?" Joe demands.

"No, but they are close."

One evening while at dinner, Joe and I meet an African American graduate student named Gerald who is researching his doctoral thesis on race relations in Cuba. Gerald has been living and traveling around the island for six months. He informs us that Cuban prisons, like prisons in America, are filled overwhelmingly with Black men and women. Black men and women, even with the social safety net, are often on the bottom of the country's economic ladder. Discrimination against Black Cubans by White Cubans still exists, and Blacks are often labeled as lazy and shiftless.

For many years after the Revolution, there was little public or governmental discussion of race. The emphasis was on improving the lives of all Cubans. Not until the 1980s were affirmative action programs introduced to re-dress historical racial inequalities. And just as the move to bring more Blacks into government and higher positions in the workforce took off, the Soviet economy collapsed, sending the Cuban economy into a tailspin because of its dependence on Russian aid. We learn that Blacks are often victims of racial profiling by the Cuban police, and Gerald, a bespectacled, burly brother from Newark, says that he has been in situations where he has felt harassed by the police because he is Black.

In the period after the Revolution, the government argued that socialism would eliminate vestiges of past racism and make its resurgence in the present impossible. What I learn from our conversation with Gerald is how crucial it was everywhere that Black people were enslaved to deal with the slave legacy and its impact on Whites and Blacks aggressively, and persistently, and to implement sustained systemic redress for Blacks immediately after emancipation. But nowhere in the Caribbean or in America did that occur. Worldwide, after emancipation formerly enslaved Blacks were met with segregation, discrimination, and myriad forms of neoslavery. One afternoon as I walk along the Malecon, the eight-mile wall along the perimeter of Havana that holds back the Atlantic Ocean, the same ocean that delivered Africans into their own holocaust, I meditate on the similarities between the African American sojourn in the New World and that of the Black and brown Cubans that pass me on my solitary stroll. If even Castro's revolution failed to heal historical racial wounds and make racial equality real, where in the world, I wonder, could it happen?

I witness the same color-code pattern in Havana that I have seen on other Caribbean islands. At our hotel, White Cubans register us at the front desk. In the restaurant, the waitstaff is White. Most of the tourists who come to Cuba each year are European, and clearly the government wants to put its whitest face forward. At our hotel the only darker-skinned male employee that we see is the doorman. The cleaning staff is mostly comprised of Black and mulatto women.

When we eat lunch or dinner in the paladares, the restaurants operated in the private homes of Cubans, the racial nature of the economy becomes even more painfully apparent. In the paladares the food is plentiful, tasty, and sumptuously prepared, much more appetizing than the meals we are offered in the government-owned hotels. During the week on the island we eat in two paladares in Havana. The White Cuban owner/hosts are gracious and friendly, and their homes are comfortable and welcoming. In both cases the families were able to establish these enterprises because of money sent to them by relatives in Miami. I suspect and Manuel confirms that very few Black Cubans have the financial resources to establish such businesses.

Manuel has been a tour guide for three years, and he tells us that he has saved a considerable sum from the tips he receives at the end of each guided tour. In Cuba the U.S. dollar is the form of currency that has the most buying power, and that essentially keeps the economy afloat. Manuel tells Joe and me that one day he wants to own his own tourist business. As the Cuban economy becomes less socialized and more capitalistic, there will be more opportunities for a greater variety of business ventures, Manuel says. He wants to be poised to take advantage of the inevitable changes in the economy.

Former Black Panther and Black Liberation Army member Assata Shakur lives somewhere on the island. In 1979 Shakur escaped from a U.S. prison where she was serving a life sentence for the murder of a New Jersey state trooper, during a gun battle between troopers and Black Panthers. A Black Panther was also killed. Shakur says that during the incident she was shot once with her hands in the air and again in the back while she was on the ground. Shakur denies killing the state trooper and has been for many years a symbol of government repression of radical liberation groups in the United States. When she escaped from prison, Shakur lived underground, then in 1984 surfaced in Cuba, where she was granted political asylum. Despite her status as a guest of the government, Assata Shakur has been a vocal critic of Cuban racism.

Santiago de Cuba is the island's second largest city and the heart of Black Cuba. Considered the "cradle" of the Revolution, Santiago de Cuba was the site of key events that influenced the course of the overthrow of Batista in 1959. A city known for its music, art, literature, and politics, it is a fusion of African, Haitian, and Spanish influences.

The city feels different from Havana, and as soon as our tour bus arrives at our hotel from the airport I am aware of more black and brown people than in Havana. When we check in at the hotel we are greeted again by White Cubans at the desk. But the narrow, sloping streets around the Hotel Casa Grande are filled with Black Cubans. Our hotel faces Parque Cespedes, a cobblestoned park with benches, which is dominated by a bronze bust of Carlos Manuel de Cespedes, who declared Cuban independence from Spain in 1868. The hotel and the park are surrounded on all sides by architectural remnants of history—the oldest house still standing on the island, built in 1522; the site of an old Spanish fort, which provides a stunning view of the harbor; a cathedral that looms over the park like the presence of God.

It is here in Santiago de Cuba that I confront the true identity of this country. The men and women hurrying past us on the narrow streets, waiting for buses, shopping in the meagerly supplied shops, are descendants of Africans who were enslaved and Spanish colonial settlers, so Cuba is both a Black and a mulatto nation. The people I see have ivory and brown to black skin, flat, wide noses, and straight hair and thin lips. They are a racial cornucopia. On the outskirts of the city are the sugar plantations, which have been harvested by brown to black people for hundreds of years and are harvested by them even now. Cutting sugar cane is as backbreaking as picking cotton. And I feel an enormous kinship with these people, many of whom look like Black folks I would see in any Black neighborhood at home.

Walking the streets of Santiago de Cuba, I am stopped several times by Black Cubans, dark-skinned men who cheerfully approach and ask if I am American. Americans are easy to spot, even when casually dressed. Our clothing is distinctive, we look better fed, we don't walk the streets like they belong to us. One man is clearly pleased to have a chance to practice his English with me and tells me that he has a cousin in New York. "He lives in Bronx. Do you know that place?" he asks, beaming. I tell him that I do know the Bronx. He stands before me, smiling, clearly pleased that he has spoken to an American tourist in English. I wonder about his cousin, if he has met with discrimination in America, if he ever longs to return to Cuba. Clearly the man standing before me envies his cousin for his arrival in what I know that this man feels is the "Land of Opportunity" despite the hostile U.S. policy toward Cuba that has so weakened the economy and made migration for many of the ambitious seem the only recourse.

In Cuba, *mulatto* is a legitimate racial designation, separate from Black and White. Many of the people I encounter in Santiago de Cuba are clearly mulatto, and I remember Manuel telling Joe that a mulatto woman from this part of the country is considered the island's ultimate symbol of female beauty. I feel so many contradictory things, wondering at the rigidity of racial classification in the United States, and how so many biracial people end up classifying themselves as Black rather than what they really are, racially mixed. I feel the attitudes about racial designation are perhaps more honest here. People are allowed to claim and take pride in everything that has influenced who they are, all the forces that have shaped them.

Yet I am disturbed as well by what we see of the darkest Black people in Santiago de Cuba. While sitting on the balcony of our hotel one evening with several members of our group, talking and sipping fruit juices and sodas, I notice an elderly White man sitting with a young Cuban girl at a table a few feet away. Several others at the table notice the couple too, and we are immediately uncomfortable and begin speculating about their relationship. I hate that we assume that the young girl must be a prostitute, but before leaving home, I read that despite the social safety net, Cuba is a poor country and that Black and mulatto women and girls are often driven into prostitution. We can hear snatches of their conversation, and the man speaks with an Italian accent. He sits puffing on a cigar, an expensive Rolex on one wrist. He has the air of a seasoned, world-weary traveler. The young girl is dark, her hair is corn-rowed, and her skimpy top and shorts are flimsy and worn. The girl looks no more than fifteen, and she sits close to the man, sipping an ice cream soda with the smile of the supplicant, of someone for sale. She is all practiced quiet laughter, and the man is unresponsive, as though it is up to the young girl to perform for him, as though he is merely a bored spectator at a show.

At my table, we do not say the word *prostitute*, or *jin-tero*, the Cuban vernacular term. We do not need to. We sit in uncomfortable silence. We sit, three African Ameri-can women saddened by the sight of another Black woman selling herself in order to survive. And when the man sum-mons the waiter and pays the bill and he and the young girl rise, they head to the elevator. I wonder where the girl lives. If she will be safe. If she will be arrested. How much the man will pay her.

Earlier in the week, while walking near the hotel, Joe was approached by two Black men who, with hands ex-tended, asked him for money. They asked Joe to give each of them five dollars. He refused to give them the money but offered to go with them to a store, where he would pur-chase for them the items they needed. At a store several blocks away, Joe purchased toilet paper, detergent, bread, milk, and sugar, which the men said they needed for their families. Joe then sat with the two men on the balcony of

our hotel after buying them sodas, and they told him of
their frustrations.

They had jobs, but the salaries were too low to live on.
One man said that he had quit his government job at a
rum factory and was trying to work for himself, hoping to
make more money that way. Joe told me that both men
pointed to the inside of the hotel and said, "All the money
that comes in the country from tourism, none of it comes
down to the people to make our lives better. More and
more tourists are coming every year, but our lives get
worse."

On the plane back to the United States I reflect on
what I have seen. More than any other recent experience,
this week in Cuba has dramatized for me that colorism is a
global phenomenon, a truly international virus. Its cruelest
impact is in the stifled opportunities and wretched lives
of its victims. I think of the contradictions—a mulatto
woman is the standard of beauty, even as blond White
Cuban women are preferred for high-profile jobs in the
country's tourist industry; the country's cultural soul is
African/Black, yet the international face of Cuba, the one
we see most often, is White. In Cuba I was forced to see
just how deeply racism and colorism are intertwined, how
they are codependent and spring from the same suprema-
cist impulse.

In this black and brown "socialist" nation I have seen
once again the persistence of white-skinned privilege, the
stubbornness of discrimination, and the marginalization of
those who are dark. But I think also of Manuel, how his

hard work and intelligence have been rewarded. I left Cuba holding on to the hope that the young prostitute and the men that Joe helped are not the only symbols of the status of Blacks in Cuba. I like to think and I pray that Manuel represents the possibilities of the present and the future.

Three months after our return from Cuba, I read that the NAACP plans to establish a branch in Havana.

Zora and Me

I am colored but I offer nothing in the way of extenuating
circumstances except the fact that I am the only
Negro in the United States whose grandfather on the
mother's side was not an Indian chief.

—ZORA NEALE HURSTON IN "HOW IT FEELS
TO BE COLORED ME"

In 1997, the Zeta Phi Beta sorority honored me with a
Woman of the Year Award. Seven years earlier, I had
founded the Zora Neale Hurston/Richard Wright
Foundation, which presents programs that discover, train,
and honor writers of African descent. The award from the
Zetas was in recognition of my writing and my literary
activism.

Accompanied by my husband, Joe, my son, Michael,
and my stepson, Austin, I spent the Sunday afternoon that
I received the award with a group of elegant, attractive, educated Black women who were trailblazers. I felt enormously gratified to be recognized by these women and
inducted as an honorary Zeta.

The first chapter of Zeta Phi Beta was organized on the campus of Howard University in 1920 and quickly became known for seeking members who were brainy and ambitious. The afternoon I received my award, I was unaware that the Zetas were considered the sorority for dark Black women and in some corners were derided and mocked because so many Zetas were brown to black. I knew only that nearly all the gracious, witty women honoring me that day were of a darker hue. Because I knew the crucial role that colorism had played in the early history of African American sororities and fraternities (for example, at their inception the Alpha Kappa Alphas and the Deltas were almost exclusively open only to light Black women), I was not surprised by what I saw.

Zora Neale Hurston, now recognized as one of America's most original and enduring literary voices, was a Zeta. When I was honored that day, I felt that the parallel paths my life and Hurston's had sometimes taken had culminated in a glorious and satisfying symbolism.

It meant everything to me when I first saw photographs of Zora Neale Hurston and saw that she was a brown-skinned woman. By the time pictures of Hurston began appearing on the jackets of her resurrected and reissued novels in the late 1970s, and early 1980s, as well as on the backs of collections of essays and literary criticism devoted to her works, I was familiar with the life, the literary legacy, and the mythology of the world-class writer.

She was a daughter of the South, born in Notasulga, Alabama, but raised in the all-Black town of Eatonville,

Florida, a town that Hurston would make illustrious. Her father, the Reverend John Hurston, was a charismatic preacher who headed several congregations in the region. Her mother, Lucy, doted on Zora and urged her daughter to "jump at de sun" in order to fulfill the enormous gifts that Lucy recognized early in Zora. In Eatonville, she was steeped in the rich traditions of Black oral and folk expression and belief.

Gazing at the photographs of Hurston, I thought of her deep and intense friendship with poet Langston Hughes, and of her independence and her sly southern humor (she coined the term "Niggerati" to describe her fellow Negro writers). She had conducted groundbreaking anthropological research in the South and in Haiti and Jamaica, using techniques that later became standard in the field. I knew that Hurston was a novelist, short story writer, journalist, playwright, and anthropologist, and that by the time of her death in 1960 much of her work was out of print and she remained obscure and little-known until the essays of Alice Walker breathed new life into Hurston's literary legacy.

I knew all this when I began seeing Zora's face—everywhere, it seemed. It was a face that heartened and encouraged me because it seemed to augur that a brown-skinned woman could in fact do what Zora had longed to do when she wrote to her patron Annie Nathan Meyer, "I am striving desperately for a toehold on the world."

A *toehold on the world*. I love that phrase. I love the way it reveals Hurston's greed for experience and achievement.

Hurston has become immensely important to me because of the way she asserted her sense of literary authority, how she invented and gave birth to herself as a woman who lived and wrote with a sense of mission. Hurston represented to me what it was possible for a brown woman to do and be. She took her rightful place on the train of life, rejecting the Jim Crow car. She made herself into the woman and the writer "who could," and I embraced Zora for many reasons, one of them being that she was a brown woman, like me.

Writing is one of the most rebellious, incendiary acts that an individual can perform. I have been writing *something* (poems, stories, articles, essays) since I could hold a pen. But it has taken years for me to define myself as and to become an author, one who imagines and creates with a sense of power and inevitability.

It did not always seem inevitable that I should write. That I would or should be read and listened to. For if I wrote, and wrote with steely determination and imagination, I would have to write my way out of the hold of the racist and colorist assumptions about brown to black Black women that I'd inherited. I would have to write my way into a consciousness that rejected Sapphire and Beulah as the ultimate symbols of my fate, even as I opened my heart to those women, my sisters.

I would have to write myself into being visible to a world dedicated to turning me into a phantom. Like most writers, I write to be heard. And I write to be loved. I write seeking congregants who will attend the church of my specific beliefs, adherents to my assertion of reality, converts to my vision. To write I would have to believe that all that was possible. I would have to write myself out of the margins and into the core of human experience. I would have to use my brown woman's attitude, my brown woman's instinct and intelligence, as keys to unlock the cosmos and see my brown woman's soul as the seed of everything that every one of us dreams. To the extent to which I have achieved any of this, the way was paved for me by Zora.

By all accounts, Zora was considered attractive. She was a stylish dresser who in the photos I have seen of her simply wore the hell out of hats, was ladylike and quite proper in white gloves, and could unveil a seductive cat's meowing smile. Zora dramatized, satirized, and ridiculed the color complex and its effects in plays like *Color Struck* and *Polk County* and in all of her fiction. She gave us the unforgettable high yellow long-haired heroine Janie Crawford in her masterpiece *Their Eyes Were Watching God*. Yet my relationship to that text has been complex and filled at times with frustration and questions about Hurston's motives and her intent. As a brown-skinned woman grateful for Hurston's ability to write about the color complex from the perspective of light and dark victims and perpetrators, I have often wondered why in a book inspired by one of Hurston's own deeply felt but unfulfilled love affairs she chose to make her alter ego a light-skinned woman. I have wondered if Hurston, for all her eccentricity and nonconformity, found it impossible to build a novel as resonant and lyrical and profound as *Their*

Eyes Were Watching God around a brown to black Black woman. A woman who looked like Zora herself.

I have read the novel half a dozen times and taught it nearly as many times as well. Each reading has revealed more about the unique ways in which Janie Crawford is both beloved and bedeviled, revered and reviled by her community, all because of her light skin and straight hair. I applaud Hurston's presentation of the tragic intricacies of the color complex in the life of Janie Crawford and in the psyche of the men who lust after her and still oppress her and turn her into an object. It took me several readings of the text to learn to truly accept Janie as my sister, to see in her life the outline of all womanhood, be it lived inside a light or dark skin. Discussion with students and others who love the book, as well as my own spiritual growth and journeys, has opened me over the years to the layered and often hidden lessons of the story.

But the question remains: Why did Zora make Janie light? *Their Eyes Were Watching God* is a magnificent novel that like all lasting literature is rooted in the soul of its hero/heroine. Although the novel is set in one southern state, Florida, the narrative feels both large and intimate, and Florida is clearly representative of all the places we live as backdrop to our quest for identity.

Was it easier for Hurston to imagine such a large female hero light rather than dark? Would readers embrace a darker heroine with the same passion that Janie inspires? These are questions that are unanswerable. But they are questions that, in the colorist society that created Hurston,

Janie Crawford, and Hurston's readers, nevertheless haunt the text.

Clearly Hurston was possessed of an indomitable will and an unshakable faith in herself that sheltered her through an often difficult life and career. She died poor but not broken in spirit. What mattered most to me as I decided quite consciously to become like Hurston, a "woman of letters," writing in various genres, was that Hurston had opened herself to and never denied her muse. She honored the good, the bad, and the ugly in "her people." I don't think that Zora desired fame as much as she hungered for a place and a way to continually express herself as griot and dream weaver.

This is the Zora Neale Hurston that I adopted as ancestor-mentor. I named the foundation I created for Hurston because she was such an outspoken, articulate protector of her vision of Black life and Black writing. She stood up to Richard Wright and defended her stories, which he called buffoonish and naive in their portrayal of Black southern experience. I took a spine-tingling delight in uniting the spirits of these two bold, authentic voices.

Zora inspired me because she was a brown-skinned woman who made the world sit up and take notice of her genius. There were other reasons too. Zora's mother encouraged and exulted in her daughter's love of reading, her education, and her solitary, reflective nature. My mother told me one day when I was fourteen, as I sat at the kitchen table watching her roll dough to make biscuits, that I was going to write books. With that fearless charge, that faith-filled prediction, my mother anointed me. Like Zora, in my mother I found perhaps one of the most important things a writer needs—permission from someone they love to venture into the unknown. Yet over the years I have warred silently, and with enormous guilt and shame, with the colorist legacy that my mother bequeathed me. That is an inheritance that threatened to but never did silence or destroy me. My mother gave me a crucible to overcome. When she anointed me as a writer, she unwittingly also gave me the tools to build, word by word, a different, accepting sense of who I am.

Like Zora, I had a stormy relationship with my father, which alternated between periods of reconciliation and recrimination. Like Zora, I loved my father with a frightening passion and loyalty that assured that our differences would be momentous, our ability to forgive each other tenuous.

Like Zora, I was cast adrift by the death of my mother and into a long period of wandering and restless searching. It was a time during which I was convinced that I was indeed a motherless child. Zora seemed to be a woman in perpetual motion, traveling anywhere and everywhere to create or find a good story or folk tale. After the death of her mother, her father moved his much younger lover into the house and bed he had shared with Zora's mother and responded to Zora's grieving outrage by asking her to leave.

My journeys from Washington, D.C., to New York, to Nigeria, and back to the United States to Boston, to Senegal, to Paris and back to Washington were part of a period of migration on which I embarked searching for adventure, love, and a sense of self that the back-to-back deaths of my parents stripped me of. I wanted to see the world, but I hoped that somewhere along the way in some village, on some boulevard, in some park, I would bump into the part of me that could finally know peace. But I learned the same lesson that James Baldwin discovered during the years of his expatriate life in Europe—that you take home with you. And in the end, like Zora I returned "home" to the place that had shaped me to settle and face the future.

So the afternoon that I became an honorary Zeta, I could feel Zora's presence in the sanctuary of the church where the program was held. She sat somewhere in the back, uncustomarily silent, her spirit completely at ease in the midst of her brown-skinned sisters. And I thought, quite surprisingly, of the term *Sapphire*, which in the street vernacular came over time to have a meaning other than a bossy domineering woman. *Sapphire* could also be used to describe a woman who was considered beautiful, desirable, as valuable as a gem. As I stood at the podium accepting my plaque, and filled with an emotion I had not expected, I gazed out at the pews filled with rows of lovely brown to black women who seemed to me then as precious as the most rare and sought-after stones. Zora was the jewel in our Zeta Phi Beta crown. Those women were Sapphires and so, thank God, was I.

Letter to a Young Black Girl I Know

This is a letter that I was not supposed to have to write. A letter that, when I was nineteen, four years older than you are now, I imagined would never be necessary again. I was a political activist who wanted to change the world. And in some very important ways, along with others storming the barricades of the status quo, I did. But in other ways the world, too much of it, remains the same. Back then I believed that black is beautiful. I believe it now. We have traveled nearly by warp speed into the present, and yet I feel that we are standing still on nearly the same spot where we once were rooted. I am writing you this letter to tell you a very simple and yet elemental thing that you as a young dark-hued Black girl must know and always cherish. You are black. And you are beautiful.

Look in the mirror. Really look at your skin. It is deep dark. It is almost black. Like your father's. Do you know how many wondrous, amazing, beautiful things in the world are the color of you? The night sky. *Think of its depth, its breadth. How mysterious and seductive it is. How when you are sitting on the front stoop on a summer night, staring into its eternity, you feel sheltered, you feel safe. Black is a regal color. If no one has ever told you this before, I am telling you now: Black is the color of queens. It is the color of kings.*

I want you to look at yourself. See the beauty of your face. But you cannot see your face, really see it, until you clear your mind. Not with your eyes, anyway. You will see it with your longings and your fears. You will see your face through the prism of I wish I was, why can't I be, if only I was, maybe one day . . . *And sweeping out the clutter, the clatter, the noise, is a thing that you can do. You are not too young. You are not too weak. You can look at yourself and see who you are and love what you see.*

Get rid of the hair fixation. Pack it up and seal the box and throw it away. You have the kind of hair that people in your mother's and father's families have had for generations. Strong. Tight. Coiled. It is the kind of hair that you are supposed to have. Hair that's in your genes. In your DNA.

And, my dear, you have short hair. Short hair, that most terrible of curses for a Black woman. I remember the press-and-curl rituals of my youth. I remember praying for long hair. For straight hair. But you are more than your hair. So much more.

You straighten your hair, and sometimes you lengthen it with extensions that give you shoulder-length braids. Those are options. But please believe me. You do not have to have braids down to your hips to be a pretty girl. I see how different you are, how you walk with so much energy and confidence when your hair is braided, when you have extensions in your hair. I see how you are slumped, how you hardly want to look people in the face, when you don't have the braids in, when your hair, your short hair, is pressed and combed back from your face. I can feel how you feel naked, exposed, and ashamed.

And of course family and friends reinforce your doubts. I was there the day Nanna brutally scolded you because your hair was not braided. It was neat but it was not braided, and Nanna scolded you as though your short hair, gleaming with a shimmering layer of Ultra Sheen, were a crime. As though you sat before her unclothed, stark and awful. Writing this, I recall our conversation about the girl in your class who wore a natural hairstyle to school, who wore her hair cut close like mine and how your classmates teased her and said she looked like a monkey. And I remember your telling me that you thought the girl looked cute but you did not have the courage to tell her that or to say it to the girls teasing her. Your classmates are afraid. Terrified, actually, of anything that reminds them of who they are. And they are afraid because their parents and so many of the people in their lives are afraid too. I never want you to be afraid of what you are. Or what you look like.

There will be enough other terrors awaiting you, terrors
that are justified, terrors that you can't control.

I am asking a lot of you. Like everyone in the
family, I want you to make good grades, go to college,
love your neighbor, contribute to the community, and I
want you to love yourself. But loving your Black self is a
task that you will have to achieve sometimes alone. On
your own, blotting out the contradictory messages of kin,
questioning the assertions of friends. I am asking a lot of
you. That's what I am supposed to do. And I ask it
knowing that you can rise to the heights I affirm for you.
Even if you cannot do it now, it is my job, my mission,
to whisper the words in your ear. Even if you don't
"hear" and understand the words for several years, you
will never answer their call unless they summon you.

The day I stood in front of the mirror and saw and
loved my face and my hair for the first time in my life I
was alone—completely, utterly alone. We are always
alone when we find the truth. The fact that we are alone
makes the taste of affirmation no less sweet.

I guess I am worrying about the hair issue because
for so many Black girls getting braids and cornrows has
less to do with having an African-inspired style than with
"getting some hair." Some hair that can be shaken and
fingered. I guess I worry because I know that our
African sister ancestors wove their hair and dyed it, and
created amazing styles within the context of an African
standard of beauty. But we have no African American

*standard of beauty, only a White-influenced standard. I
care less about what you do with your hair than what
you think of yourself. But I insist that you know and
believe that short hair, natural hair, is as beautiful on
you as your extensions or a perm. And I worry when I
see four- and five-year-old girls insisting on extensions
because already at that tender age they know, because
we have told them, that unless they have thick, long hair
they are not beloved.*

*Maybe one day I will take you to the Smithsonian
Museum of African Art. We'll stroll through the
museum and look at the variety of images of Africa, of
African women and men created by ancient,
anonymous, and contemporary famous artisans. I have
a wonderful photography book with pictures of Black
women from different parts of the world. We can sit and
look at the pictures. Talk about them. No, I won't make
it a test (smile), and I promise I won't judge your
responses. I want you to know that there is a universe of
Black women, past and present, that you are related to,
and many of them reflect your specific black beauty.*

*And you will have to find your voice. You will have
to respond if you are teased because you are dark.
Because your hair is short. You have to challenge
ignorant, self-hating remarks. You have to assert your
value and your pride. Even if you don't always feel
valuable and proud, and there will be days like that,
assert it anyway. That assertion, honored regularly, will
turn the words into reality.*

*You have to forgive people with colorist attitudes.
You can't change everyone. And what's most important
is how you see yourself. That you see your own beauty
and worth. We have to stop believing in the color
complex and passing it from generation to generation.
You have to help us make the world a safe and loving
place for girls who look like you. And women who look
like me.*

*I write you this letter to begin a conversation, not to
lay down the law. I am your elder, but I expect you to
show me the way. When I was four years older than you
and believed anything was possible, I believed that black
is beautiful. I still do.*

*Love,
Marita*

Acknowledgments

There are many many people to thank for their support and cooperation in the creation of this book. I want to thank those who spoke so openly and honestly with me about their memories and experience of the color complex. Their stories and revelations taught me much and enlarged my sense of the significance of this project. I want to thank my husband, Joe Murray, for our many conversations about this subject, which helped me to develop my ideas and perspectives, and I want to thank him for being my soul mate and friend. Clyde McElvene kept asking tough questions and gave me the gift of his remembrances and his conscious perspective. TaRessa Stovall and Kathleen Halley gave me much to think about in their response to early drafts. My agent, Carol Mann, once again proved to be wise and wonderful and my editor, Janet Hill, kept nudging me to write from my secret secret place. Her enthusiasm and perception kept me going and kept me writing. I thank Steve Rubin and everyone in my Doubleday family for their continued support.

Printed in the United States
by Baker & Taylor Publisher Services